ISLAND HARVEST

ISLAND HARVEST

Nick Nairn

Photographs by Jean Cazals

west 175
publishing

West 175 Productions
P.O. Box 84848
Seattle, WA 98124
Web site: www.greatfoodtv.com

West 175 Production Team
Publisher: Greg Sharp
Americanization Editor: Alison Leach
Design Director: Barbara Schmitt
Copyeditor: Cynthia Sharp

This book is published to accompany the television series entitled
Great Food which was first broadcast in 2000.

thirteen
WNET NEW YORK

ISBN 1-884656-10-2
Printed in Hong Kong

The quote on page 6 is reproduced by the kind permission
of Faber & Faber Limited

This book was first published to accompany the television series
Island Harvest, which was produced by Ideal World Productions
Limited for BBC Scotland.

UK Version Published by BBC Books, BBC Worldwide Limited,
Woodlands, 80 Wood Lane, London W12 0TT
First published 1998
© Nick Nairn 1998
The moral right of the author has been asserted.

Photographs by Jean Cazals, © BBC Books 1998

Commissioning Editor: Nicky Copeland
Project Editor: Khadija Manjlai
Copyeditor: Christine King
Art Director: Frank Phillips
Designer: Isobel Gillan
Stylist for photography: Antonia Gaunt
Home Economist for photography: Debbie Major

Dedicated to Bunty

ACKNOWLEDGMENTS

I'd like to thank all the folks at Ideal World, especially
Hamish Barbour, Peter Jamieson, and Carl Hindmarch for
making *Island Harvest* such a cracking series. Special
thanks to Debbie Major for all her help with testing the
recipes and for being able to read my writing; Fiona
Buchanan, my long-suffering assistant, for allowing me to
meet my deadlines; Andrew Meehan for his continuing
creative inspiration; and the team at BBC Books, notably
Nicky Copeland, Frank Phillips, and Khadija Manjlai.

A Personal Note from Nick Nairn About Beef on the Bone
*"Although there has been major concern over sales of beef
on the bone, my opinion of the government's blanket ban is
that it is a knee-jerk reaction. No differentiation has been
made between native cattle, farmed organically by small
producers, and intensively reared continental breeds,
which are not fed naturally and have to be overwintered
and fed on pellets and grain. Should the ban be reversed,
I would urge everybody, everywhere, to buy the beef of
such native cattle as Aberdeen Angus, Galloway or
Shorthorn – sturdy wee coos fed on grass. Ultimately,
though, the decision rests with you, the consumer."*

Previous page: *Seared Scallop Phyllo Tartlets with Basil,
Tomato, and Caramelized Onion* (page 32)

CONTENTS

INTRODUCTION

How's your carrot?
It's a carrot.
So much the better, so much the better.

Waiting for Godot, Samuel Beckett

It shows how far we've all come when a self-taught chef like me can harp on in public and in print, and not be hounded out of the place in a hail of couscous, Puy lentils, and half-eaten banana tarte tatins. But, it seems, we're no longer preaching to the unconvertible.

There's a real sense of change pulsing through Scottish food culture. Chefs all over the country are getting hold of the best raw produce they can find and working wonders with it – which shouldn't be too hard, as what makes Scottish cooking unique is what makes it universal: fine produce. After all, you don't have to be a person of consequence to make the best out of good ingredients.

I'm under no illusions, however. Some people continue to torture some of the finest food on the planet into the most illogical shapes and daffy combinations. Of course, some things will never change. During the filming of the TV series on which this book is based, I tasted some pretty dodgy food served in restaurants and hotels which, having access to such good produce, should know better. But let's leave them to it. Welcome to *Island Harvest*.

I can't think of anything finer than messing about in boats off the west coast of Scotland. You've just had a steaming plate of *Razor Shell Clam Risotto*, the sea is so blue you want to wear it, and the sky is bathed in that lambent, smoky light you don't get anywhere else. Dreadful things could be happening in the world and you just can't work it up to care. You're in heaven.

So, what's changed this time around? Well, cooking on a boat can be a tricky situation at the best of times. Add the nervous energy of a television crew and you're guaranteed to be pumping adrenalin. We held our own though, and the ideas within these pages are, I think, the most straightforward and my best yet. Alongside the likes of *Roast Loin of Hare on Truffled Spinach with Horseradish Mash* is *Harissa Chicken with Couscous and Lemon and Cumin Yogurt*. They draw on different traditions but I'm not yoking together disparate cultures for the sake of it; this is fusion food.

But you can also take the low road and head for the homemade oatcakes or *Mull Cheddar Omelet*. There's no secret formula or magic potion. Good food shouldn't be treated like a Fabergé egg. *Island Harvest* is a compendium of all the things I enjoy about cooking – informality, spontaneity, and generosity. I've also tried to combine the attributes of ingenuity and simplicity, classicism and open-mindedness. I hope you enjoy the results.

Salmon Sushi (page 33)

USEFUL EQUIPMENT

Getting yourself quality gear means saving time and effort on the day, so it's worth treating yourself – even if you have to do so in installments.

Blowtorch This is a perfect tool for finishing off crème brûlées and roasting red bell peppers and tomatoes, but you can of course get by with a broiler.

Cast-iron griddles A ridged griddle, or stove top grill pan, is great for roasting vegetables and getting that criss-cross chargrilled effect on meat and fish. Smooth griddles are excellent for making scones. It's best to get good, heavy-bottomed ones, preferably with metal handles so that they can go in the oven as well.

Cheese grater (râpé) Brilliant for chocolate or fresh Parmesan. You can keep the cheese in the grip at the top and store the whole thing in the refrigerator.

Crockery It's much easier to make food look attractive on big white plates. Don't spend a fortune on crockery and have the food looking cluttered on the plate because of the pattern. Let the food speak for itself.

Cutting boards Ten years ago the environmental health people said that we should use plastic cutting boards rather than wooden ones. Plastic boards are terrible! They blunt your knives and they retain the smell of food, so they taint what you're chopping. Now the health police have relented, thank goodness, but here are a couple of hints regarding wooden boards: wipe them down but don't put them in the dishwasher as they warp. A wet dish towel under the board when you're using it keeps it firmly in place and nice and level.

Electric whisk A hand-held one gives you more control than a mixer when you're making things like meringue. It's also easier to clean than a mixer and it saves you bulging, aching biceps.

Electronic scales For precision measuring. Commercial kitchens cover them loosely in plastic wrap and use them as normal. This stops all the debris of the kitchen getting into the gubbins of the scales.

Food processor Indispensable for soups, pasta, breads, pesto, breadcrumbs…the list goes on and on. It really takes a lot of the hard graft out of cooking. The only drawback is that they are a bit fiddly to clean, so I only use one for medium or large batches of food.

Garlic press A good-quality nonstick one. I used to hate them, but actually they're quite useful.

Hand-held blenders Also known as "stick-liquidizers," these small electric blenders have revolutionized sauce-making, allowing anyone to make light, frothy sauces and banishing "split" sauces to a thing of the past.

Knives Spend the most money that you can afford on knives. A large 10–12 inch (25–30 cm) knife, a flexible boning knife, and a steel for sharpening will aid your cooking no end. Learning how to use the steel takes practice but it's essential for maintenance of your blades. Hold the steel upright with your hand behind the guard and put the base of the knife at the base of the steel at an angle of 20 degrees. Using long strokes, pull the knife up the steel so you go from base-to-base in contact, to tip-to-tip in contact. Then turn the knife over and do the same on the other side. The steel sets up an electromagnetic force that realigns all the molecules at the edge of the blade – and it just takes any wee dings out. You're stopping the knife from going blunt, you're not sharpening it. Once a knife is blunt, a steel won't sharpen it.

Le Creuset terrine This is a wonderful piece of kitchen equipment. I prefer Le Creuset terrines over any other because they are cast iron, which means they don't warp, they conduct heat evenly around the whole terrine, and they will last you through to the next ice age! All the ingredient quantities for terrines in this book are based on a Le Creuset terrine capacity.

Mandolin graters Plastic versions are a good introduction to using mandolins but, if you can afford it, try and get a Braun mandolin – it's the one that professional chefs use and it does cost mega-bucks (about $175), but it's possibly one of the most useful tools in the kitchen. Watch your fingers though, and fling away that last bit of food unless you want to incorporate your fingertips in the dish that you're making.

Omelet pan An 8 inch (20 cm) pan makes a perfect-size omelet for one and it's also useful for dry-roasting small amounts of spices. Get one with a nonstick surface and a heavy bottom if you can.

Pasta machine Indispensable for fresh pasta. If you don't use your machine regularly, then oil the rollers, otherwise they will seize up. Use a wee bit of vegetable oil for this, not WD 40! On the same note, the first time you use the machine, put through a disposable batch of dough as there's always oil on the rollers which will taint your first lot of pasta.

Pastry cutters Much beloved of the presentation brigade, myself included. They are great for creating the beautiful towers of food that we love so much.

Pepper grinder To get a really good pepper grinder, look for one that has a Peugeot mechanism in it…they're the best by miles.

Plastic spatula or spoonula Great for scraping every little bit from mixing bowls. It will pay for itself in months.

Preserving jars These swing-top jars with replaceable rubber seals are handy for storing pesto, home-dried tomatoes, and practically anything else you can cram into them. Just make sure you wash and dry them well before use.

Rolling pin I prefer the plastic ones because they don't stick so much and don't dent so easily.

Seasoned baking sheets Like pots and pans you should consider this as an investment – the more you bake with it, the more like an old friend it will become. Treat it well and it will last forever (or nearly). Look for a flexible silicon mat, a nifty little piece of equipment that chefs use for brandy snaps and biscuits, etc. You can get one from cookshops and some supermarkets now. Nothing sticks to the mat, but it won't stop things burning if you're not looking out for them.

Sieves The chinois is a fine, metal, conical sieve. Very handy for straining stocks, sauces, and sorting out any lumpy sauce (yes, even for me, folks!). To get the best from your chinois, wash it as soon as you've used it, otherwise all the holes clog up and it becomes knackered. A conical strainer with larger holes is great for sieving mashed potatoes and straining soups and, although quite expensive, lasts for ever.

Skillets The best ones to use are cast iron. After being seasoned they are superb for cooking with – and they last forever. As well as these you can get really good-quality, stainless steel, nonstick pans. Never buy a cheap nonstick pan because the nonstick surface will come off in bits in an outrageously short time, so buy the best you can afford.

Sushi mat A handy wee tool for making sushi. You can get them from most Chinese supermarkets and they cost only a couple of dollars or so. They are made from thin strips of bamboo woven together into a flexible mat, designed specifically for rolling perfect cylinders of sushi and that's what sushi is all about: perfection.

Wok A wok is the best and safest thing to use for deep-frying. Its sloping sides mean that the oil can expand outward when it gets hot. Steep-sided pans give the oil nowhere to go except up – very tricky!

Other useful pieces of equipment include: a good-quality lemon zester, a canelle cutter, measuring cups, a set of ramekins, metal or glass mixing bowls, a waiter's friend (one of those nifty all-in-one corkscrews that is shaped like a pen knife), and a little coffee grinder for grinding spices.

CUPBOARD INGREDIENTS

Having the right things in your cupboard makes it much easier to throw together an excellent meal with hardly any warning. You've got to admit it's far nicer to come home and have something delicious, rather than a piece of frozen chicken and a can of baked beans.

In your refrigerator

Bulb of garlic Fresh is preferable, and is usually available in early season, around April.

Butter (unsalted), which also freezes well. Many butter producers mark notches on the wrapper so that you know how much to cut without worrying about cups.

Chilies Supermarkets generally have a heat scale on packs of chilies as a guideline, but the trick is to keep tasting what you're making all the way through, so you can't go wrong.

Eggs If you can get your hands on eggs straight from a farm where the chooks run round free, you are in luck. The difference in quality between these eggs and even supermarket free-range eggs is huge: the yolks are a fantastic orange color, and the flavor is something else. Once you've tried them, you'll never look back.

Fresh herbs, which keep for up to four or five days in the little trays that you get them in. If you can, though, have some growing. They make such a difference to the flavor of a dish. Rosemary, thyme, and mint all grow like wildfire if you give them a chance.

Fresh ginger root

Home-dried tomatoes (see page 184)

Lemons and limes

Pesto

Reggiano parmesan cheese Get a nice block of it.

Tapenade

White wine A couple of bottles are always handy.

In your freezer

Butter Unsalted.

Olive oil Freeze some in an ice-cube tray. Little cubes of unctuous flavor.

Pesto Freezes well in the same way, and the cubes don't lose their color.

Pine nuts Strangely, this is the best place to keep them fresh.

Stock Homemade or purchased. Supermarkets are increasingly producing good-quality, fresh stocks that keep very well in the freezer.

In your cupboard

Balsamic vinegar Buy the best you can afford.

Black and white peppercorns The important thing to remember about pepper is that it must, must, must be freshly ground. The pre-ground stuff is too fine and it goes stale very quickly.

Bouillon cubes Chicken bouillon cubes are good all-rounders for emergencies – try and use the best quality you can find. They're really good for dishes such as risotto which is finished with lots of highly flavored ingredients that would mask the taste of fresh stock.

Cans of chopped tomatoes

Cans of precooked legumes Cans of chickpeas, kidney beans, or lima beans just take the hassle out of 24 hours of soaking. Give them a good rinse under the faucet before you use them, though, as the liquid they're kept in is full of sugar and salt.

Chili and black bean sauce This stuff packs a punch! You can get it from Chinese supermarkets. Try and get the proper Chinese version as it has a much better flavor.

Chocolate Look for one with a minimum of 60 percent cocoa solids.

Curry pastes Good-quality ones.

Dark soy sauce I find Kikkoman's is good.

Dried egg or rice noodles Those 4-minute ones are great.

Dried pasta

Flour Self-rising, all-purpose and whole wheat.

Gelatin Envelopes of powdered gelatin, or leaf gelatin if you can find it.

Honey Use the clear, runny type.

Maldon salt In most of my recipes you'll see that Maldon salt is almost ubiquitous. I prefer it above processed salt and coarse sea salt because the soft flakes of Maldon give lovely frissons of flavor in your mouth – they really have that iodide flavor of the sea. (Maldon is a town in Essex, England where this salt is harvested from a nearby river estuary.)

Olive oil Really you want to have two kinds of olive oil: one cheaper kind for general use, and a really top-notch one, preferably an estate oil from a single producer. The good-quality oil, with its deep color and rich, peppery flavor, is perfect for dressing salads and drizzling around dishes like risotto.

Red wine vinegar Preferably Cabernet Sauvignon vinegar.

Rice Arborio and basmati.

Spices Paprika, chili, saffron, whole nutmegs, cinnamon, cloves, star anise, cumin and coriander seeds, turmeric, etc. I buy whole seeds and grind them myself in a coffee grinder when I need them. This serves two purposes: it stops them going stale so quickly and it also lets you get full flavor out of them by dry-frying them whole before you use them.

Sugar Natural brown sugar, such as muscovado, has much more flavor than white. Also keep confectioners', granulated, and superfine sugar.

Sunflower oil

Tabasco

Thai fish sauce This is made from fermented fish and, used in small quantities, it adds a piquant flavor to a dish.

Tomato ketchup Add it to tomato sauces for sweetness – it balances the acidity of the tomatoes.

Wine It's always nice to have a few bottles of wine knocking around in the kitchen as they can add a wonderful dimension to some dishes – and of course you'll have something to sip while you're cooking. Never cook with wine you wouldn't drink yourself, so you just need to find another use for that Matteus Rosé your Aunt Hilda gave you for Christmas last year. I usually have a couple of bottles of red Burgundy and Californian Chardonnay in my store-cupboard, but for some reason they never seem to last long.

Worcestershire sauce

NOTES ON RECIPES

Before you start using this book, please note the following:

- Eggs are large unless otherwise stated. Buy farm-fresh eggs laid by chickens allowed to run around free. The difference in quality between these eggs and even supermarket free-range eggs is huge: the yolks are a brilliant orange color and the flavor is exceptional.

- At the time of going to press, the British government had just introduced a ban on the sale of beef on the bone. This book, therefore, contains recipes using beef on the bone. See also author's note on page 4.

- Spoon measurements are level.

- Conversions are approximate and have been rounded up or down. In a few recipes it has been necessary to modify them very slightly. Follow one set of measurements only; do not mix metric and American.

- Oven temperatures and cooking times are flexible and may vary according to the equipment and ingredients used.

- Wash all produce before preparation.

Scotland's lush land – sometimes

bathed in sunlight, at times washed

by soft rain – produces some of the

world's best crops; even the weeds

hold great promise.

SOUPS

NETTLE SOUP

with warm soda scones

This was a real revelation when I tasted it made by Heather Dewar in her tiny cottage overlooking the Sound of Jura. The secret is to use just the tips of young nettles – strong gloves and sharp scissors are a must here. The finished soup has got a lovely mineral flavor – and no, it doesn't sting your lips!

Serves 4

¼ cup butter
1 large onion, chopped
1 lb (450 g) potatoes, peeled and diced
1 large leek, cleaned and sliced
2½ cups Chicken Stock (see page 181)
1 lb (450 g) young nettles
Maldon or sea salt
freshly ground white pepper
4 tablespoons crème fraîche

For the soda scones:

1¾ cups (225 g) all-purpose flour
1 teaspoon baking soda
1 teaspoon cream of tartar
½ teaspoon Maldon or sea salt
scant 1¼ cups buttermilk, or fresh milk soured
    with a little lemon juice

Bring a large pan of water to a boil. Melt the butter over a low heat in a second pan. Add the onion, potatoes, and leek, and cook gently for 10 minutes until softened. Add the stock and bring to a boil. Cover and leave to simmer for 15–20 minutes until the vegetables are just cooked. Meanwhile, put on a pair of rubber gloves and pick the nettle leaves from their stalks. Wash them well, drop them into the pan of boiling water, and cook them for just 60 seconds. Drain them immediately and refresh under cold water. Squash them into a food processor and blend into a smooth purée. Tip this into a pitcher and set aside.

For the scones, heat a smooth griddle over a medium–high heat. Sift the flour, baking soda, cream of tartar, and salt into a bowl. Gradually stir in enough buttermilk or milk to make a moist, but not wet, soft dough. Turn out the mixture onto a surface lightly dusted with flour and shape into a round about 1 inch (2.5 cm) thick. Cut this into 4 or 6 wedges. Lift them onto the griddle and cook them gently for 10–15 minutes on the first side until golden brown. Turn them over and cook them for another 5 minutes. Keep them warm.

Purée the soup until smooth. Return it to the rinsed pan, stir in the nettle purée, and season to taste with salt and pepper. Reheat the soup gently but do not let it boil or you will lose its beautiful, vivid green color. Serve in warmed soup bowls with a spoonful of crème fraîche in each and the warm soda scones.

LIMA BEAN SOUP

with chili and deep-fried chorizo

This majors on big robust flavors and uses my favorite legume, the underrated lima bean, which makes a gorgeously creamy base for this soup. The parsley, lemon, and garlic mix which you bung in at the end is in fact the classic Italian flavoring called gremolata. Normally it's added to osso bucco, but here it brings all the other flavors alive with its tangy freshness. Use thin slices of big chorizo for the garnish so they end up a bit like big meaty potato chips once fried. (Got that idea from eating a pepperoni pizza on the way back from the pub one night. I picked off all the crispy sausage and binned the stodgy base – amazing where we chefs get our inspiration.)

Serves 6-8

1½ (225 g) dried lima beans

⅔ cup olive oil

2 onions, peeled and chopped

4 cloves garlic, crushed

2 teaspoons harissa or minced red chili
  peppers from a jar

1 teaspoon paprika powder

½ teaspoon ground cumin

a good pinch of saffron stamens

6½ cups (1.5 liters) Chicken Stock
  (see page 181)

2 fresh bay leaves

finely grated zest of ½ small lemon

3 tablespoons chopped fresh flat-leaf parsley

2 tablespoons lemon juice

Maldon or sea salt and freshly ground
  black pepper

sunflower oil for deep-frying

18–24 very thin slices chorizo sausage

a little extra-virgin olive oil, to serve

Cover the lima beans with plenty of cold water and leave to soak overnight. The next day, heat the olive oil in a large pan. Add the onions and fry for about 10 minutes until soft and golden. Add half the crushed garlic and the harissa or chili and fry for another 2 minutes.

Add the paprika and the ground cumin and fry for 1 minute, stirring. Drain the beans and add to the pan with the saffron, chicken stock, and bay leaves. Bring to a boil, cover and leave to simmer for 45 minutes, or until the beans are very soft.

Mix the remaining garlic with the lemon zest and the chopped parsley. Stir this mixture into the soup and purée in batches until smooth. Return to the pan and add the lemon juice with some salt and pepper to taste. Keep hot over a low heat.

For the garnish, pour about 1 inch (2.5 cm) of sunflower oil into a pan and heat to 350°F (180°C). Separate the chorizo slices and fry a few at a time for about 15 seconds until crisp and lightly golden. Lift out with a slotted spoon and drain on paper towels.

Spoon the soup into warmed soup plates and pile some of the deep-fried chorizo slices into the center of each bowl. Drizzle the soup with a little extra-virgin olive oil and serve.

CHILLED CUCUMBER AND YOGURT SOUP

with seared langoustines

This is a beautiful soup for a warm summer's day – tasty, refreshing, and pretty to look at too. It also uses my favorite combination of hot and cold in the same dish. You could serve it with or without the langoustines, or substitute raw tiger shrimp instead. Make sure that the stock isn't too strong or it will overpower the other more delicate flavors – the tubs of ready-made supermarket chicken stock are perfect for this recipe.

Serves 4

2½ cucumbers
1¼ cups Greek natural yogurt
1¼ cups Chicken Stock
  (see page 181)
5 tablespoons crème fraîche

a few drops of Tabasco Sauce
Maldon or sea salt
2 tablespoons chopped fresh mint, chervil,
  chives, or dill, or a mixture if you prefer
6 langoustine tails
2 tablespoons olive oil

Peel 2 of the cucumbers, cut them in half lengthwise and scoop out the seeds with a melon baller or teaspoon. Roughly chop the flesh into small pieces and liquidize in batches in a blender or food processor with the yogurt, chicken stock, crème fraîche, Tabasco Sauce, 1 teaspoon salt, and herbs until really smooth. Pour the soup into a bowl, cover with some plastic wrap and chill in the refrigerator until very cold.

Bring a large pan of lightly salted water to a boil. Add the langoustine tails, bring them back to a boil and then drain. Refresh in cold water. When they are cool enough to handle, peel off the shells and cut them in half lengthwise. Peel the remaining cucumber, cut it in half, and scoop out the seeds. Cut the flesh in long, thin ribbons and dry them on some paper towels.

Just before you are ready to serve, heat the olive oil in a large skillet. Add the langoustine halves and stir-fry over a high heat for 1 minute until just cooked. Season with a little salt.

Ladle the soup into large, chilled soup bowls and pile some of the cucumber ribbons into the center of each bowl. Arrange 3 of the hot langoustine halves on top of each portion and serve.

EMERALD GREEN POTATO AND WATERCRESS SOUP

The great things about this soup are its bright green color and earthy, slightly metallic flavor which you achieve by adding the watercress at the end of cooking, thereby keeping both its color and its flavor. The idea was stolen from my friend Paul Rankin, an Irish wonder-chef and a man who really understands food. He's still a big Irish galoot though! While on the subject of plagiarism, the idea of adding the spinach at the end of cooking belongs to another pal, Phil Vickery, a lad who can cook a bit and is an arch rival on *Ready Steady Cook*. I wish he'd stop beating me!

Serves 6

¾ cup butter

1½ lb (675 g) floury main-crop potatoes, such as Idaho, peeled and thinly sliced

7½ cups (1.75 litres) boiling water

3 cups (350 g) watercress, stalks and all, roughly chopped

2 oz (50 g) spinach, washed and any large stalks removed

Maldon or sea salt and freshly ground white pepper

6 tablespoons heavy cream and watercress sprigs, to garnish

Melt the butter in a large pan. Add the potatoes and stir well so that they all get well coated in the butter. Cook over a very gentle heat for about 6 minutes until they are slightly softened and starting to break up. Then increase the heat, add the water, and bring to a boil. Cover and leave to simmer for 20–30 minutes until the potatoes are very soft.

Stir in the watercress and cook for just 3 minutes. Stir in the spinach and, as soon as it has wilted into the soup, purée it (in batches if necessary) until smooth. Return to the pan, season with salt and plenty of ground white pepper, and bring back up to temperature.

Pour the soup into heated serving bowls and garnish each portion with the cream and a couple of sprigs of watercress.

SPICY EGGPLANT AND TOMATO SOUP

with minted yogurt

Eggplants love spices and tomatoes, so this soup's off to a great start. The minted yogurt garnish tempers things a bit and provides that much-loved (by me) temperature contrast. Use a good-quality curry paste as hot or as mild as your taste prefers. Personally I've come to love the combination of cilantro and basil – a real East meets West thing – but you could use just one or the other with equal success.

Serves 6-8

2 large eggplants, weighing about 8–10 oz (225–275 g) each

1¼ cups olive oil

2 red onions, peeled and sliced

1 tablespoon cumin seeds

2 teaspoons coriander seeds

1 tablespoon hot curry paste

2 teaspoons fennel seeds, finely ground

3 cloves garlic, crushed

1 (14 oz) (400 g) can chopped tomatoes

5 cups (1.2 litres) boiling water

Maldon or sea salt and freshly ground black pepper

2 tablespoons chopped fresh cilantro

2 tablespoons shredded fresh basil

For the minted yogurt:

6 tablespoons natural low-fat yogurt

1 clove garlic, crushed

1 tablespoon chopped fresh mint

Cut the eggplants into ¾ inch (2 cm) thick slices. Heat ¼ cup of the olive oil in a large pan. Add a layer of eggplant slices and fry for a few minutes until lightly browned. Then turn them over, add a splash more oil, and fry once more until golden. Lift out onto a plate and repeat with the rest of the eggplants and some more of the oil, until they are all cooked.

Now add the remaining oil and the red onions to the pan and fry for 5 minutes until soft and lightly browned. Meanwhile, heat a dry skillet until quite hot. Add the cumin and coriander seeds and toss them around for a few seconds until they darken slightly and start to smell aromatic. Tip them into a coffee grinder or mortar and pestle and grind them to a fine powder. Add the curry paste, roasted cumin and coriander, and the ground fennel to the onions and fry for 2 minutes, stirring now and then. Add the garlic and cook for 1 minute.

Roughly chop the eggplants and return them to the pan with the chopped tomatoes and the water. Bring to a boil, cover and leave to simmer for 20 minutes.

Now you need to purée the soup in batches until smooth. Return it to the pan and stir over a high heat until heated through. For the minted yogurt, simply mix everything together with a pinch of salt. Check the seasoning of the soup and stir in the chopped cilantro and basil. Pour it into warmed soup bowls and serve garnished with a good spoonful of the minted yogurt.

MUSSEL AND SAFFRON SOUP

I know this has been done before but it's too good not to give you my version. You need two things for success here – good fat mussels and real saffron stamens – funny, that! In previous versions I've puréed this soup, but here the mussels have been left whole so that you can appreciate their lovely texture. However, if your mussels are a bit below par, then puréed them is probably the best option. Use enough saffron to give the soup a nice color, but not so much that you can't taste anything else.

Serves 6

3¼ lb (1.5 kg) fresh mussels
2½ cups dry white wine
¼ cup butter
2 leeks, cleaned and finely chopped
2 stalks celery, finely chopped
1 carrot, peeled and finely chopped

2 cloves garlic, finely chopped
a good pinch of saffron stamens
2½ cups heavy cream
cayenne pepper
Maldon or sea salt
2 tablespoons finely chopped fresh chives

Scrub the mussels well, scrape off any barnacles, and pull out the beards protruding from between the two closed shells. Discard any that won't close when they are lightly tapped on the work surface.

Heat a large pan over a high heat. Bung in the mussels and the white wine, cover and cook, shaking the pan every now and then, for 3–4 minutes, or until the mussels have opened. Discard any that stay closed.

Tip the mussels into a colander set over a large bowl or another pan and then pass the cooking liquid once more through a chinois or very fine sieve and reserve it. Set aside half of the mussels and remove the meats from the remainder.

Melt the butter in the pan you used for the mussels. Add the chopped vegetables and the garlic and cook over a medium–high heat for a few minutes until the vegetables are tender. Add the reserved mussel liquid (except for the last spoonful or two which might contain some sand) and the saffron and leave to simmer for 10 minutes.

Add the cream and bring the soup back to a boil. Add the mussel meats and mussels in their shells, cayenne pepper, and a little salt if needed, and simmer for about a minute until the mussels have heated through. Stir in the chopped chives, spoon the soup into warmed bowls, and serve straightaway.

PARTAN BREE

"Partan" is a traditional Scottish name for crab and "bree" means gravy. So this is "crab gravy," a name that doesn't do this gorgeous soup justice. Using rice to thicken the soup was a big thing in Victorian times and it is still good. When buying crabs, look for a big, heavy monster which will mean less work for more meat. Failing that, you could use frozen or pasteurized crabmeat but you won't get the same intensity of flavor as using fresh.

Serves 6

¼ lb (1.75 kg) cooked crab
2½ cups Chicken Stock (see page 181)
⅓ cup long-grain rice
2½ cups whole milk
1 teaspoon anchovy essence

8 drops of Tabasco Sauce
Maldon or sea salt and freshly ground
    white pepper
2 cups cream
a pinch of ground mace
cayenne pepper and chopped fresh chives,
    to garnish

Remove both the brown and white meat from the crab, setting aside the larger pieces of white meat from the claws for garnishing the soup. Put all the pieces of crab shell into a pan with the chicken stock, bring to a boil, and leave to simmer for 15 minutes. Meanwhile, put the rice and the milk into another pan, bring to a boil, and simmer for 15–20 minutes until the rice is tender.

Strain the crab-flavored stock through a muslin-lined sieve into another pan. Stir all the crabmeat except the claw meat (you should have about 1 lb/450 g) into the rice and milk mixture and purée until smooth. Then stir this into the pan containing the stock, together with the anchovy essence, Tabasco, and some seasoning to taste. Bring gently up to a boil, stir in the cream and the mace, and leave until not quite boiling.

Spoon the soup into warmed bowls and garnish with the reserved claw meat, a sprinkling of cayenne pepper, and a few chopped chives.

SPICY BUTTERNUT SQUASH SOUP

with coconut milk and cilantro

The flavor idea comes from Thai cooking, where spicy flavors are partnered with sweetness (here the chilies with the squash and coconut milk) and often cut with the acidity of lime, ginger, and lemon grass. The secret is in the balance, with no one element dominating, so make sure you taste as you go. It's important to find nice ripe squash – not as easy as it sounds since the hard shells prevent you from feeling how squidgy the inside is – so it's best to make friends with a grocer in the know.

Serves 6

2 tablespoons peanut or sunflower oil

1 onion, chopped

2 lb (900 g) butternut squash

3¾ cups Chicken Stock (see page 181) or
    Marinated Vegetable Stock (see page 179)

1 (14 fl oz) (400 ml) can coconut milk

3 tablespoons chopped fresh cilantro

juice of 1 lime (about 2 tablespoons)

For the red curry paste:

2 cloves garlic

2 inch (5 cm) piece ginger root, peeled and
    chopped

2–3 long, thin red chilies (depending on how
    hot you like things), seeded and chopped

1 stalk of lemon grass, outer leaves removed
    and the core chopped

1 teaspoon ground coriander

1 teaspoon turmeric powder

finely grated zest of 1 lime

1 tablespoon chopped fresh cilantro

First make the red curry paste. Simply put all the ingredients into a food processor and blend to a smooth paste.

For the soup, heat the oil in a large pan. Add the onion and fry gently for about 10 minutes until it is very soft and nicely browned. Meanwhile, halve and then peel the butternut squash, scoop out the seeds, and cut the flesh into small chunks.

Add the curry paste to the onions and fry, stirring now and then, for 2 minutes. Add the pieces of squash to the pan with the chicken or vegetable stock and simmer for 30 minutes until the squash is nice and tender.

Purée the soup (in batches if necessary) until smooth. Return it to the pan, stir in the coconut milk, and leave to simmer gently for another 5 minutes. Add the cilantro and lime juice and stir for just 1 minute. Ladle into warmed soup bowls and serve straightaway.

RAGOUT OF HEBRIDEAN SHELLFISH

This recipe is a bit "cheffy", not to mention expensive, but if you want a "meaty" soup dish to die for, it's this. You do need seriously fresh, quality shellfish and the optional caviar for maximum impact. So, OK, prepare to sell your soul, put the kids out to work, and get on down to a good fishmonger. Having made this investment, don't blow it by overcooking the shellfish. They really need only 2 minutes to cook.

Serves 4

12 langoustine tails
1 small lobster tail
2 lb (900 g) large fresh mussels
¾ cup dry white wine
¾ cup dry vermouth
1 ¼ cups Fish Stock (see page 180)

1 ¼ cups heavy cream
a squeeze of fresh lemon juice
Maldon or sea salt and freshly ground
   white pepper
6 large scallops, cleaned
2 tablespoons caviar (optional)
sprigs of fresh chervil, to garnish

Drop the langoustine and lobster tails into a pan of boiling water, bring back to a boil and then drain. When the tails are cool enough to handle, break open the shells and remove the meats. Cut the lobster meat into 4 neat pieces.

Scrub the mussels well, scrape off any barnacles, and pull out the beards protruding from between the two closed shells. Discard any that won't close when they are lightly tapped on the work surface.

Place the mussels in a large pan with the white wine, cover and cook over a high heat for 3–4 minutes until they have opened. Discard any that don't open. Tip the mussels into a colander set over a bowl to collect the cooking liquor. Set aside 12 of the nicest-looking mussels for the garnish and remove the meats from the remainder.

Pour the vermouth into a medium-size pan and leave it to boil rapidly until it has reduced to about 2 tablespoons. Add the fish stock and all but the last tablespoon of the mussel cooking liquor (which might contain some sand) and boil until reduced by three-quarters. Add the cream and bring back to a boil. Taste the sauce and season with a little lemon juice, salt and pepper.

Cut the scallops in half and add them to the sauce with the langoustine, lobster, and mussel meats. Bring the sauce up to a gentle simmer and cook for 1–2 minutes. Lift the shellfish out of the sauce and arrange them attractively in the center of 4 warmed serving bowls. Take the sauce off the heat and stir in the caviar, if using. Spoon the sauce over the shellfish and garnish with the reserved mussels and the sprigs of fresh chervil.

CULLEN SKINK

(smoked haddock, potato, and chive soup)

Another traditional Scottish soup and one that's stood the test of time. It's vital to use top-quality, undyed smoked haddock to get the true flavor. The stuff from R. & R. Spink in Arbroath is the best I've tasted and I believe they now supply some of the big British supermarkets.

Serves 4-6

12 oz (350 g) floury main-crop potatoes, such as Russets, peeled and cut into chunks
4 tablespoons butter
1 onion, chopped
1 lb (450 g) Finnan smoked haddock fillets

1¼ cups water
Maldon or sea salt and freshly ground black pepper
2½ cups milk
1 tablespoon chopped fresh chives
4 tablespoons heavy cream

Cook the potatoes in lightly salted boiling water for 20 minutes. Meanwhile, melt half the butter in a large pan. Add the onion and cook it gently for about 7 minutes until it is soft but not browned. Cut the smoked haddock fillets into large pieces and add them and the water to the onions. Bring up to a simmer, cover and leave to cook for 10 minutes, until the fish is just cooked through. Lift the fish onto a plate and, when it is cool enough to handle, break it into large flakes, discarding any skin and bones. Reserve the cooking liquor.

Drain the potatoes and mash them until smooth. Now press them through a sieve – this will give an even smoother finish to the soup – and beat in the rest of the butter and some salt and pepper.

Whisk the mashed potato into the cooking liquor until the texture is smooth and creamy and then stir in the milk. Bring up to a simmer, cover and leave to cook for 3–4 minutes. Stir in the flaked fish, chives, and cream, and season to taste with a little more salt and pepper if necessary.

KIDNEY SOUP

When I was a wee boy, canned kidney soup (Grannie's, I think) and hot buttered toast were a treat on coming home from school that I've never forgotten, and this recipe attempts to recapture that taste. Unlike most of my soup recipes, this one needs good stock, preferably homemade or the bought supermarket stuff, but not cubes.

Serves 6

12 oz (350 g) lamb's kidneys

3 tablespoons sunflower oil

2 small stalks celery, finely chopped

2 medium onions, finely chopped

2 carrots, peeled and finely chopped

5 tablespoons all-purpose flour

7½ cups (1.75 liters) good lamb or Beef Stock (see page 182)

1½ tablespoons tomato paste

2 fresh bay leaves

2 sprigs of fresh thyme

Maldon or sea salt and freshly ground white pepper

3 small medium-thick slices white bread, crusts removed

3 tablespoons Clarified Butter (see page 183), warmed

1 tablespoon chopped fresh parsley

Halve the kidneys and snip out the cores with scissors. Set aside 4 of the halves and finely chop the rest. Heat the oil in a large pan. Add the celery, onions, and carrots, and cook over a medium heat for 10 minutes until soft and lightly browned. Add the chopped kidney and fry for 2–3 minutes; then lower the heat, stir in the flour, and cook for 1 minute. Take the pan off the heat and gradually stir in the stock. Stir in the tomato paste, bay leaves, thyme sprigs, and some seasoning, and bring to a boil, stirring. Cover and leave to simmer for 30 minutes.

Meanwhile, preheat the oven to 400°F (200°C). Cut the bread into ½ inch (1 cm) cubes and toss them with half of the warm clarified butter. Spread them out on a baking sheet and bake them in the oven for 5–7 minutes until crisp and lightly browned. Remove from the oven and set aside.

Remove the bay leaves and thyme sprigs from the soup and blend a quarter of it (about 2 cups/450 ml) until smooth. Return this to the pan containing the rest of the soup and bring back to a gentle simmer. Fry the reserved kidney slices in the rest of the clarified butter for about 1 minute on each side until they are lightly browned and just cooked. Lift them onto a cutting board and cut them into small, neat dice. Taste the soup for seasoning and serve in warmed bowls sprinkled with the diced kidneys, croûtons, and chopped parsley.

The cold, deep, clear waters

around Scotland's rugged coastline

yield are, without doubt, our richest

harvest: fish and shellfish of an

almost unbelievable quality.

STARTERS

SEARED SCALLOP PHYLLO TARTLETS

with basil, tomato, and caramelized onion

Not really tarts – the phyllo discs just provide a nice crispy base for the sweet, seared scallops and the rather delicious tomato, basil, and onion dressing. Do use scallops that haven't been soaked in water to plump them up and make them taste of – well, water. Frozen ones are just as bad. Big, "hand-dived" scallops are what you want every time. If cash is tight, halve the number of scallops that you use and double the amount of dressing, rather than waste money on the larger quantity of dud scallops.

Serves 4

10 large sheets of phyllo pastry
olive oil
2 large onions, thinly sliced
6 plum tomatoes

4 tablespoons lemon juice
¼ cup fresh basil leaves, torn into small pieces
Maldon or sea salt and freshly ground
  white pepper
8 large scallops, cleaned
1 tablespoon balsamic or red wine vinegar

Preheat the oven to 350°F (180°C). Stack up the sheets of pastry and cut out four 6 inch (15 cm) rounds using an upturned bowl as a template. Separate them into individual discs. Brush each one with a little of the oil and lay them out in pairs, one disc on top of another, giving them some wrinkles so that a more attractive finish is achieved. Place on a baking sheet a few at a time and bake for 8–10 minutes until crisp and golden. You should end up with 20 double-thickness discs of pastry. Remove and leave to cool. These can be made hours or even days in advance and kept in an airtight tin if you wish.

Heat 4 tablespoons of oil in a pan. Add the onions and cook over quite a high heat, stirring frequently, until they are soft and nicely caramelized. Meanwhile, peel the tomatoes – with a blowtorch or with boiling water – then seed them and cut them into very neat dice. Mix them with 3 tablespoons of oil, 1 tablespoon of the lemon juice, the basil, and some seasoning. Set aside.

Pat the scallops dry with some paper towels. Detach the corals (roes) and save them for another dish. Cut each white scallop meat into 3 discs. Heat a large skillet until it is quite hot. Add 2 tablespoons of oil and the scallop slices and sear over a high heat for 1 minute on one side only until richly browned and crispy. The slight rawness of the uncooked side will give them an excellent, sensuous texture. Do this in batches if your skillet is not very large. Remove them to a plate and season with the rest of the lemon juice and some salt and pepper.

Stir the caramelized onions into the tomato and basil mixture with the vinegar. Stack 5 discs of phyllo pastry on each plate and spoon on the tomato and onion mixture. Overlap 6 scallop slices over the top of each one and serve straightaway while the pastry is still crisp.

SALMON SUSHI

With a bit of practice, making sushi isn't that hard. But make sure you've got proper Japanese sushi rice and that you rinse it really well. You can use any kind of fish but it must be very fresh. You can make vegetarian variations too using mango, avocado, cucumber, and green onion. Sushi rolls (illustrated on page 7) can be made up to 24 hours in advance, covered in plastic wrap and sliced at the last moment.

Serves 6

Scant 2 cups Japanese sticky rice
2½ cups water
2 tablespoons superfine sugar
1 teaspoon Maldon or sea salt
4 tablespoons rice vinegar
5 sheets of dried nori seaweed
6 oz (175 g) thin salmon fillet, skinned and
*   cut into long thin strips*

3 teaspoons wasabi paste or powder, plus
*   extra to serve*
15 fresh chives, cut into long pieces

To serve:
2 tablespoons Japanese pickled ginger juice
4 tablespoons Japanese soy sauce
1 oz (25 g) Japanese pickled ginger

Put the rice into a sieve and wash it under running cold water, working your fingers through the grains until the water runs clear. Drain the rice and put it into a pan with the water. Bring quickly to a boil; then turn the heat down low and cook for 10 minutes. Remove from the heat, cover and leave undisturbed for 10 minutes. This timing is crucial to produce the correct consistency for the sushi.

Stir the sugar and salt into the vinegar until dissolved. Turn the rice out into a bowl and stir the vinegar mixture into it, fanning the rice as you do so to cool it and produce a sheen.

For sushi rolls, place a sheet of seaweed on a sushi mat (see page 10). Spread two-thirds of it with a ⅓ inch (7 mm) thick layer of the rice, leaving a clear strip down one long edge. Lay a strip of the salmon lengthwise down the center of the rice and spread it with a little of the wasabi. If you are using wasabi powder, first mix it to a smooth paste with a little cold water. Add a few chives, then dampen the clean edge of the seaweed sheet with a little water. Using the mat to help you, lift up one long edge and roll the seaweed into shape, sealing it into a secure roll with the dampened edge. Cut the roll across into ¾ inch (2 cm) lengths. Repeat with the remaining sheets of seaweed. Cut one end of some rolls at an angle if you wish.

To present the sushi, mix the pickled ginger juice with the soy sauce and pour it into a small dipping saucer. Arrange a small pile of pickled ginger, a teaspoon of wasabi paste, the sushi and the saucer of sauce on a large plate and serve.

SALMON NIÇOISE TARTLETS

A twist on a classic combination of ingredients, these tartlets not only taste great but look stunning with all the different colors showing through the egg. You can make the pastry shells up to 24 hours ahead, and the raw shells can be frozen for up to 3 weeks. Prepare the bits and pieces for the filling ahead and pour on the egg mix just before baking. The tartlets are great on their own or with a few dressed salad leaves.

Serves 6

4 oz (100 g) skinned salmon fillet

Maldon or sea salt and freshly ground
   black pepper

2 oz (50 g) green beans, topped and tailed

12 small cherry tomatoes

4 oz (100 g) cooked small new potatoes

12 pitted black olives

2 tablespoons chopped fresh basil

2 farm-fresh eggs

5 tablespoons heavy cream

2 teaspoons balsamic vinegar

2 tablespoons finely grated Parmesan

For the pastry:

2¼ cups all-purpose flour

a pinch of Maldon or sea salt

4½ tablespoons chilled butter, diced

4½ tablespoons chilled lard or vegetable
   shortening, diced

1½ tablespoons very cold water

1 medium farm-fresh egg white

For the tartlet shells, sift the flour and salt into a food processor and add the butter and lard. Process until the mixture looks like fine breadcrumbs. Transfer to a bowl and stir in the water until the mixture starts to stick together in small lumps. Gently bring it together into a ball and knead once or twice on a lightly floured surface until smooth. Divide the dough into 4 pieces and use to line four loose-bottomed tartlet pans 4½ inch (11 cm) wide × 1½ inch (4 cm) deep. Slide them into the refrigerator and leave them to chill for 20 minutes.

Preheat the oven to 400°F (200°C). Line the pastry shells with crumpled pieces of wax paper (for a better fit) and baking beans and bake for 11 minutes. Remove the paper and beans and bake the shells for another 6–9 minutes. Now brush the base of each case with a little of the unbeaten egg white and return them to the oven for 1 minute. Remove them from the oven and set aside.

To prepare the filling, cut the salmon into ¾ inch (2 cm) strips and season with a little salt and pepper. Cut the beans into 1 inch (2.5 cm) pieces and blanch them in boiling salted water for 2 minutes. Drain and refresh under cold water. Cover the cherry tomatoes with boiling water, leave for a few seconds, then drain and cover with cold water. Peel off the skins. Cut the new potatoes and olives lengthwise into quarters.

Arrange the salmon, beans, tomatoes, potatoes, olives, and basil in each tartlet shell so that all the bits are visible and stick out above the rim of the pastry. This will help to give the finished tarts an attractive appearance. Mix the eggs with the heavy cream, balsamic vinegar, Parmesan, and a little seasoning. Pour the mixture over the filling and bake in the oven for about 20 minutes, or until they are just set in the center and lightly browned. Carefully lift the tartlets out of the pans and serve while they are still warm.

BUTTERFLIED LANGOUSTINES

with baby bok choy

Chili and black bean sauce is found in most Chinese supermarkets and there seem to be a hundred different varieties available. Only experimenting will tell you which is best. You really need fresh (that means alive!) langoustines, but you could use raw tiger shrimp instead. It's just that langoustines have such an incredible flavor. Be careful not to overcook them – always err on the side of underdone or you lose the texture, which should be yielding not rubbery.

Serves 4

20 uncooked langoustines or whole
   jumbo shrimp
3 tablespoons good-quality dark soy sauce
1 tablespoon clear honey
1 tablespoon Dijon mustard

2 tablespoons freshly squeezed lemon juice
5 tablespoons sunflower oil
12 oz (350 g) baby bok choy, trimmed
1 tablespoon chili and black bean sauce
2 tablespoons roughly chopped fresh cilantro
Maldon or sea salt and freshly ground
   black pepper

Butterfly the langoustines or shrimp by cutting them in half lengthwise through the shell, keeping them attached at the tail end. Mix the soy sauce with the honey, mustard, and 1 tablespoon of lemon juice. Pour into a shallow dish, toss in the shellfish, and marinate for 1 hour.

Preheat a barbecue or broiler to medium–high. Cook the langoustines or shrimp for 3–4 minutes, turning them over halfway through. At the same time, heat the oil in a large pan. Add the bok choy and stir-fry over a high heat for 1–2 minutes. Add the rest of the lemon juice, the chili and black bean sauce, cilantro, and seasoning and toss together well.

To serve, pile the bok choy into the centers of 4 warmed plates and arrange the langoustines or shrimp around it.

ARBROATH SMOKIE CROQUETTES
with a spicy tomato salsa and balsamic vinegar syrup

You might not think croquettes are very sexy, but the big flavor of the smoked haddock and the spiciness of the salsa make this into a dish worthy of its own star billing. The croquettes can be frozen once breaded. Defrost them overnight in the refrigerator on paper towels. The Balsamic Vinegar Syrup (extravagant, but worth it) keeps for months in a sealed bottle.

Serves 6

1½ lb (675g) floury main crop potatoes
1 tablespoon butter
2 lb (900 g) Arbroath smokies or lightly
    smoked small haddock
1–2 tablespoons heavy cream
Maldon or sea salt and freshly ground
    white pepper
sunflower oil for deep-frying
3 tablespoons all-purpose flour, seasoned
    with ½ teaspoon Maldon or sea salt and
    some pepper

1 medium farm-fresh egg, beaten
1½ cups fresh white breadcrumbs
Balsamic Vinegar Syrup, to serve
    (see page 183)

For the spicy tomato salsa:

6 small vine tomatoes, peeled and seeded
1 small red onion, peeled and quartered
1 long, thin red chili pepper
1 large clove garlic, cut into slivers
2 teaspoons lemon juice
a handful of fresh cilantro leaves
2 tablespoons olive oil

For the croquettes, peel the potatoes and cut them into chunks. Cook in boiling salted water until tender. Drain well, tip back into the pan, and mash with the butter until smooth. Press through a sieve with a wooden spoon to make a very smooth purée and leave to cool a little bit. Meanwhile, skin and bone the Arbroath smokies and break the flesh into small pieces. You should be left with about 3 cups (350 g) of flaked fish. Add the flaked fish, cream, and a little salt and pepper to the potatoes and mix well. Divide the mixture into 12 and form into barrel shapes. Place on a baking sheet, cover with plastic wrap and chill for 20 minutes.

For the salsa, cut the tomatoes into arc shapes, cut the onion lengthwise into thin slices, and cut the chili across into thin slices (removing the seeds if you wish). Put them all in a bowl with the garlic and stir in the lemon juice and some seasoning. Cover and chill.

Pour some oil into a pan until it is about one-third full and heat it to 350°F (180°C). Dip the croquettes into the seasoned flour, the egg, and then the breadcrumbs, pressing the breadcrumbs on well to give a thick, even coating. Cook the croquettes, 4 at a time, for about 4 minutes until crisp and golden. Lift each batch out onto some paper towels and keep warm in a low oven. Stir the cilantro leaves and olive oil into the salsa. Place 1 or 2 croquettes on each plate and pile the spicy tomato salsa alongside. Drizzle a little of the balsamic vinegar syrup around the edge of each plate and serve while the croquettes are still hot and crunchy.

BAKED SHRIMP SOUFFLÉS

with a saffron mayonnaise

This might seem like a waste of good tiger shrimp – but wait until you taste these light, little fishy clouds with the saffron mayonnaise melting into them to form a liquid center. Actually, the Chinese quite often grind shrimp for making things such as shrimp toasts and shrimp balls, so I feel vindicated in turning them into soufflés.

Serves 6

1 tablespoon butter

½ cup fresh white breadcrumbs

¼ cup finely grated Parmesan

6 oz (175 g) raw shelled tiger shrimp

2 farm-fresh egg yolks

Maldon or sea salt

¼ teaspoon cayenne pepper

⅔ cup heavy cream

4 farm-fresh egg whites

½ teaspoon freshly squeezed lemon juice

For the saffron mayonnaise:

a pinch of saffron stamens

1 farm-fresh egg yolk

1 teaspoon lemon juice

¼ teaspoon Maldon or sea salt

⅔ cup olive oil

⅔ cup sunflower oil

a few drops of Tabasco Sauce

For the mayonnaise, put the saffron stamens into a mortar and pestle and grind to a fine powder. Tip the powder into a small bowl (use a pastry brush to make sure you get all the powder out). Add the egg yolk, lemon juice, and salt, and whisk together well. Now very gradually whisk in the oils until the finished mixture is thick and silky smooth. Whisk in the Tabasco and a little more lemon juice to taste if you wish. Cover with some plastic wrap and chill until needed.

For the shellfish soufflés, all the ingredients must be very cold before you start. Slide a baking sheet onto the middle shelf of the oven and preheat it to 425°F (220°C). Generously grease six 3 inch (7.5 cm) ramekins with the butter. Mix the breadcrumbs with the Parmesan and shake some around in each ramekin until the bottom and sides are well coated.

Put the raw shrimp into a food processor and blend for a few seconds. Add the egg yolks, ½ teaspoon salt, and the cayenne pepper, and blitz once more until smooth. Add the cream and blend for no more than 10 seconds. Scrape the mixture into a large bowl. In another large bowl, whisk the egg whites with a good pinch of salt and the lemon juice until they form stiff peaks. Gently fold one large spoonful of the egg whites into the shrimp mixture and then gently fold in the remainder.

Spoon the mixture into the ramekins and slide them onto the baking sheet. Bake for about 10–12 minutes until risen and golden brown. Make a small slit in the top of each one, drop in a teaspoonful of the saffron mayonnaise and serve immediately.

RAZOR SHELL CLAM RISOTTO

with peas, bacon, and mint

This unlikely sounding dish works really well as the sweetness of the clams and peas matches the saltiness of the bacon and Parmesan, and the mint adds a nice clean flavor. You could use scallops or langoustines instead of razor shell clams, which can be a tad difficult to find. In fact, the risotto is fabby enough to be served on its own. As always with risotto, use the best arborio rice and Parmesan available. The stock, however, is just dandy made from a good-quality bouillon cube.

Serves 4

1½ lb (675 g) razor shell clams, scrubbed
    clean
1½ cups dry white wine
about 3¾ cups Chicken Stock (see page 181)
5 tablespoons olive oil
4 slices rindless streaky bacon, chopped
1 onion, finely chopped
1 clove garlic, finely chopped

1¼ cups arborio rice
¾ cup peas, fresh or frozen
4 tablespoons butter
¼ cup finely grated Parmesan, plus extra to
    serve (optional)
2 tablespoons chopped fresh mint, plus extra
    to serve (optional)
Maldon or sea salt and freshly ground
    white pepper

Place the razor shell clams and ⅔ cup of the white wine in a large pan. Cover and cook over a high heat for a few minutes until the clams have opened. Discard any that remain closed. Tip them into a colander set over another bowl and, when they are cool enough to handle, remove the meats from the shells and cut them into fine dice. Pour all but the last tablespoon of the cooking liquid (which might contain some sand) into a measuring pitcher and make up to 3¾ cups (900 ml) with the chicken stock.

Heat the olive oil in a large pan. Add the bacon, onion, and garlic, and stir-fry over a medium heat until the bacon has lightly browned and the onion has become translucent. Add the rice and stir it around for a couple of minutes until it has become well coated in the oil. Add the rest of the white wine and simmer for another 4–5 minutes, stirring, until almost all the liquid has been absorbed by the rice. Now lob in half the stock and bring up to a boil, stirring. Reduce the heat to a simmer and leave the risotto to cook until the stock has been absorbed. Add the rest of the stock and continue to cook, stirring occasionally, until the rice is tender but with a little bite left in it, and the texture is rich and creamy. This should take about 20 minutes in all.

Now stir the peas into the risotto with the butter, Parmesan, diced razor shell clams, and mint. Season to taste with salt and pepper and cook for 2 minutes. Spoon into 4 warmed serving bowls and sprinkle with a little more cheese and a bit more chopped mint if you wish.

Mussels

One of the things that I keep banging on about is to remember that recipes are just guidelines and in most cases are to be mucked about with or personalized. So the next four recipes are a variation on a theme, that good old bistro staple, moules à la marinière.

STEAMED MUSSELS

with chili, red onion, tomato, and basil

In this first version the flavoring comes from the southern Mediterranean, so you get lovely tomato, garlic, and basil flavors with the heat of the chili spicing things up.

**Serves 4
(or 2 as a main course)**

2 lb (900 g) fresh mussels

2 tablespoons extra-virgin olive oil, plus a little extra to serve

2 cloves garlic, very finely chopped

½ medium red onion, very finely chopped

1 finely chopped long, thin red chili pepper, seeds left in if you like things hot

¼ cup dry white wine

4 well-flavored tomatoes, skinned, seeded and chopped

4 tablespoons chopped fresh basil

freshly ground black pepper

2 teaspoons lemon juice

Maldon or sea salt

a loaf of fresh ciabatta bread, to serve

Scrub the mussels well, scrape off any barnacles, and pull out the beards protruding from between the two closed shells. Discard any that won't close when they are lightly tapped on the work surface.

Put the olive oil, garlic, onion, and chili into a large pan, and cook over a gentle heat for 5 minutes until the onion is just soft. Add the white wine, chopped tomatoes, and mussels; cover and cook over a high heat, giving the pan a good shake every now and then, for 3–4 minutes until the mussels have opened.

Uncover the pan and discard any mussels that are still closed. Add the basil and plenty of freshly ground black pepper, then taste the sauce and add the lemon juice and a little more salt if necessary. Turn the mussels over once or twice to distribute the basil evenly and then spoon them into large, warmed soup bowls. Drizzle over a little more olive oil and serve with chunks of ciabatta bread.

STEAMED MUSSELS

with a lemon, cream, and parsley sauce

This version is closer to the original but the cream makes it richer and the lemon zest gives it a fabby tang – I'm dribbling now!

Serves 4
(or 2 as a main course)

2 lb (900 g) fresh mussels
2 tablespoons butter
4 large shallots, peeled and very
    finely chopped
1 clove garlic, very finely chopped

¼ cup dry white wine
⅔ cup heavy cream
finely grated zest of ½ small lemon
3 tablespoons chopped fresh flat-leaf parsley
about 1 tablespoon lemon juice
Maldon or sea salt and freshly ground
    black pepper
crusty French bread, to serve

Scrub the mussels well, scrape off any barnacles, and pull out the beards protruding from between the two closed shells. Discard any that won't close when they are lightly tapped on the work surface.

Melt the butter in a large pan. Add the shallots and garlic and cook gently for about 3 minutes. Add the wine and the mussels, cover and cook over a high heat, shaking the pan every now and then, until the mussels have opened. Discard any that remain closed.

Remove the pan from the heat and lift the mussels out with a slotted spoon into a large bowl. Keep them warm. Return the pan to the heat and boil the remaining cooking liquor rapidly for 6 minutes until reduced and well flavored. Add the cream and lemon zest and continue to boil for 4 minutes, stirring continuously to prevent the sauce from sticking, during which time it will thicken slightly. Add the chopped parsley and some lemon juice, salt and pepper to taste. Return the mussels to the pan and turn over in the sauce for a minute or two until heated through. Spoon into large, warmed soup bowls and serve with chunks of crusty French bread.

STEAMED MUSSELS

with chili and black bean sauce

Off to the Orient for inspiration here. The results of this recipe should be fresh and fragrant flavors with the ginger, green onions, and soy all doing their thing together. Make sure you use light sesame oil, and if you like, you could sprinkle over some toasted sesame seeds at the end and serve with some cooked noodles. Yum!

Serves 4
(or 2 as a main course)

2 lb (900 g) fresh mussels
4 green onions, trimmed
1 tablespoon peanut or sunflower oil
2 teaspoons sesame oil, plus extra for serving
1 clove garlic, very finely chopped

½ inch (1 cm) piece fresh ginger root, peeled
  and finely chopped
1 tablespoon chili and black bean sauce
2 tablespoons rice wine vinegar mixed with
  2 teaspoons superfine sugar
1 tablespoon dark soy sauce
2 tablespoons roughly chopped fresh cilantro

Scrub the mussels well, scrape off any barnacles, and pull out the beards protruding from between the two closed shells. Discard any that won't close when they are lightly tapped on the work surface.

Cut the green tops off each green onion and slice them into long, fine shreds. Thinly slice the remaining white parts. Heat the peanut oil and 2 teaspoons of sesame oil in a large pan. Add the white parts of the green onions, the garlic and ginger, and stir-fry for 2–3 minutes. Add the chili and black bean sauce, the mussels, rice wine vinegar dressing, and soy sauce. Cover and cook over a high heat for 3–4 minutes, shaking the pan every now and then, until the mussels have opened. Discard any that remain closed.

Add the chopped cilantro and most of the shredded green tops of the green onions to the pan and turn everything over once or twice. Ladle the mussels into warmed soup bowls, drizzle over a little more sesame oil, and serve sprinkled with the remaining green onion shreds. If you are serving this with cooked noodles, remove the mussels from the pan with a slotted spoon after you have added the cilantro and green onion tops, and add the noodles to the sauce. Warm them through, divide them among the bowls, and then spoon the mussels on top.

STEAMED MUSSELS

with garam masala, coconut milk, and basil

Thailand is the source of the sweet-spicy-tangy flavor sensation in this recipe. Get the balance right here and you're in food heaven.

Serves 4
(or 2 as a main course)

2 lb (900 g) fresh mussels

1 tablespoon peanut or sunflower oil

2 cloves garlic, finely chopped

½ inch (1 cm) piece fresh ginger root, peeled and finely chopped

1 stalk of lemon grass, outer leaves removed and the tender core finely chopped

1 chopped long, thin red chili pepper, seeds left in if you like things hot

2 teaspoons garam masala

1 tablespoon Thai fish sauce

2 teaspoons palm or light brown sugar

2 tablespoons lime juice

½ cup coconut milk

2 tablespoons very finely shredded fresh basil

1 tablespoon chopped fresh cilantro

Scrub the mussels well, scrape off any barnacles, and pull out the beards protruding from between the two closed shells. Discard any that won't close when they are lightly tapped on the work surface.

Heat the oil in a large pan. Add the garlic, ginger, lemon grass, chili pepper, and garam masala, and fry for 3–4 minutes. Add the fish sauce, sugar, lime juice, and coconut milk, bring up to a boil and reduce for 3 minutes. Add the mussels, cover and cook over a high heat for 3–4 minutes until they have opened. Discard any that remain closed.

Add the basil and cilantro to the pan and turn over the mussels once or twice. Ladle them into warmed soup bowls and serve straightaway.

NETTLE PASTA

with a clam vinaigrette

I'm rather proud of this here dish, as it was made up on the spur of the moment during the filming of the TV series. Sometimes the best ideas come when your back is up against the wall, which is just what happened to your intrepid chef when he realized – too late – that he had planned to film a dish containing clams, which he had never cooked before. Silly boy! However, desperation produced this and it was pronounced a winner (by me and the rest of the crew at least). There you go, just because you're on the "telly" doesn't mean you always know what you're doing!

Serves 4

4 good (gloved) handfuls of nettle tips
2¼ cups all-purpose flour
2 medium farm-fresh eggs
2 medium farm-fresh egg yolks

For the clam vinaigrette:
4 lb (1.75 kg) cockles or small (Manilla) clams
   in their shells, scrubbed clean
4 tablespoons red wine

3 shallots, finely chopped
1 clove garlic, finely chopped
6 tablespoons olive oil
3 tablespoons chopped mixed fresh basil,
   cilantro and chives
Tomatoes Concassées (see page 184),
   use 4 tomatoes
1½ tablespoons Cabernet Sauvignon or
   another good-quality red wine vinegar
freshly ground white pepper
1 tablespoon butter

For the pasta, drop the nettle tips into a pan of well-salted boiling water, drain immediately and refresh under cold water. Squeeze dry by hand or in a clean dish towel. Put the flour into a food processor, turn on the machine, and then add the eggs, egg yolks, and nettles through the lid. Whizz for 2–3 minutes until the mixture looks like fine breadcrumbs (it shouldn't be dusty, nor should it be a big, gooey ball). Tip the mixture out onto a work surface, form into a ball, and knead for 1 minute. Cover the dough in plastic wrap and chill for 1 hour if you have time.

Cut the chilled dough in half. Flatten each piece with a rolling pin to a ¼ inch (5 mm) thickness, fold it over, and roll it out, refolding and rolling it 7 times until you have a 3 × 7 inch (7.5 × 18 cm) rectangle. It is important to work the dough until it is nice and shiny as this gives it a good texture.

If you have a pasta machine, start with it at its widest setting and pass the dough through the rollers. Repeat this process, decreasing the roller setting each time you pass the dough through until you reach the penultimate setting. Pass the dough through once more at this setting and then leave it to dry for 5 minutes. Finally, set the machine on its finest cutters (for spaghetti) and pass

the dough through. If you do not have a pasta machine, simply roll out the pasta on a floured work surface with a rolling pin until you have a ⅛ inch (3 mm) thickness. Roll the sheet of pasta carefully into a cylinder and cut this into thin strips with a sharp knife to give you spaghetti. Unroll each slice into a strand as you cut, otherwise the pasta will stick together. Drop the pasta straightaway into a large pan of boiling salted water, bring it back to a boil, and cook for 2½ minutes. Drain the pasta, drop it into a bowl of cold water to stop it cooking, then drain once more and set aside.

For the clam vinaigrette, soak the clams in several changes of water to ensure that all the sand has come out of them. Discard any that won't open when given a sharp tap. Place them in a large pan with the red wine, cover and cook over a high heat, giving the pan a good shake every now and then, for 4–5 minutes, until they have opened. Discard any that remain closed. Tip into a colander set over a bowl to collect the cooking liquor. Pour all but the last tablespoon of the liquor (which might contain some sand) back into a clean pan and add the chopped shallots and garlic. Leave to simmer for 10 minutes until the liquor has reduced to about 6 tablespoons and the shallots have softened. Add the oil and leave it to infuse over a low heat for 5 minutes.

Meanwhile, remove the clams from their shells. Add them to the shallot mixture with the chopped herbs, tomatoes, vinegar, and some freshly ground white pepper (but no salt). Place the butter and 2 tablespoons of water in a large pan. As soon as the butter has melted and the water is simmering, add the pasta and toss it around every now and then until it has heated through. Twirl each portion of the pasta onto a large roasting fork and then lift each "tower" into the center of each serving bowl. Spoon around the clam vinaigrette and serve immediately.

PEPPERED TUNA CARPACCIO

with a spicy lentil salad in a soy vinaigrette

Some people are a bit funny about eating raw fish, which is fair enough: I hate tripe! So if you are such a person, move onto another recipe because this is essentially raw fish. It's got a lovely spicy crust and the lentil salad lends some earthy texture, but it's still nice, shiny, raw tuna – yum!

Serves 6

2 tablespoons dark soy sauce

1 tablespoon Dijon mustard

1 tablespoon clear honey

2 tablespoons sunflower oil

8 oz (225 g) loin of tuna taken from a large
    fish, well trimmed

2 tablespoons Szechwan peppercorns

1 tablespoon Maldon or sea salt

a good pinch of Chinese five-spice powder

sprigs of fresh cilantro, to garnish

For the spicy lentil salad:

1¼ cups green Puy lentils

2 thin slices fresh ginger root

3 cloves garlic, peeled

1 medium red onion, very finely chopped

1 long, thin red chili pepper, seeded and very
    finely chopped

3 tablespoons chopped fresh cilantro

2 tablespoons rice wine vinegar, or white wine
    vinegar mixed with 1 tablespoon sugar

4 tablespoons sunflower oil

1 tablespoon Japanese soy sauce

Mix together the soy sauce, mustard, and honey, and pour into a small shallow dish. Heat a large skillet until it is very hot. Add the oil, then sear the tuna over a high heat, turning it from time to time, until it has cooked all over to a depth of about ¼ inch (5 mm). Transfer the tuna to the soy mixture, turning it over occasionally, and leave until cold.

Meanwhile, heat a dry, heavy-bottomed skillet over a high heat. Add the peppercorns and toss for a few seconds until they darken slightly and start to smell aromatic. Tip them into a mortar and coarsely crush them with the pestle. Stir in the salt and five-spice powder, then sprinkle the mixture onto a plate. Lift the tuna out of the marinade and dip it in the spices so that they form a thin, even coating. Cover the fish tightly in plastic wrap and chill for 24 hours.

For the salad, bring a pan of lightly salted water to a boil. Add the lentils, ginger, and a whole clove of garlic, and leave them to simmer very gently for 20 minutes until just tender. Do not have the water bubbling too vigorously or the lentils will start to fall apart.

Drain the lentils, discarding the ginger and garlic, and leave to cool. Finely chop the remaining garlic and stir it into the lentils with the other salad ingredients. Leave to go cold.

To serve, remove the tuna from the refrigerator and unwrap it. Slice the loin across into very thin slices using a long, very sharp knife. Spoon the lentils into the center of each plate, cover with 3–4 slices of the tuna, and serve garnished with sprigs of fresh cilantro.

BARBECUED MACKEREL KEBABS

with aloo bhaji

So you think mackerel is a bit oily, a cheap fish fit only for bait? Try this and I guarantee you will change your mind! Mackerel loves spices and because it has a bit of extra oil in its flesh, it means it doesn't dry out under the intense heat of the barbie. If you can't face barbecuing, then simply sear the kebabs on a cast-iron stove top grill pan, but to achieve mackerel nirvana get a barbecue and stick it on the back doorstep. The mackerel must be dead fresh – less than 24 hours old – or else you'll have oily old fish fit only for bait! And if you can't be bothered with the aloo bhaji, simply push the kebabs into pita bread that you've warmed through on the grill, pull out the skewer, and enjoy.

Serves 4

2 medium-sized mackerel, filleted and cut into
    1 inch (2.5 cm) pieces
Maldon or sea salt and freshly ground
    white pepper
dressed salad leaves and big wedges of
    lemon or lime, to serve

For the marinade:
1 long, thin red chili pepper, finely chopped
    (seeds and all)
2 cloves garlic, finely chopped
finely grated zest of 1 lemon

juice of ½ lemon (about 1½ tablespoons)
1 tablespoon chopped fresh cilantro
2–3 tablespoons olive oil

For the aloo bhaji:
12 oz (350 g) potatoes
2–3 tablespoons sunflower oil
½ teaspoon cumin seeds
½ green chili, seeded and very finely chopped
½ teaspoon ground cumin
¼ teaspoon cayenne pepper
¼ teaspoon turmeric powder
¼ teaspoon garam masala

Set up the barbecue before you start preparing the ingredients. This way, the coals will have time to become beautiful red embers that give off the perfect heat for searing the mackerel. If you are using wooden, rather than metal, skewers, this is the time to put them in water to soak so that they don't burn on the barbecue and taint the flavor of the fish.

Combine all the marinade ingredients together in a large glass bowl and season. Mix in the fish so that it's completely coated in the marinade and leave to stand for half an hour for the fish to absorb maximum flavor.

Meanwhile, peel the potatoes and cut them into 1 inch (2.5 cm) cubes. Partially cook them in boiling salted water for 7 minutes, then drain well and leave to go cold. Heat the oil in a large skillet. Add the potatoes and fry them over a medium heat for about 7–10 minutes, turning them over now and then, until they are light golden brown. Sprinkle over the cumin seeds and the chopped green chili and continue to cook for 3–5 minutes. Then sprinkle over the ground cumin, cayenne pepper, and turmeric powder, and cook for another 5 minutes, turning the potatoes as they fry so that they get coated in a rich, spicy crust. Sprinkle over the garam masala and some seasoning and toss together well. Keep warm.

Thread the pieces of fish onto the skewers and whack them onto the barbecue for about 5 minutes on the first side. Baste them with a little of the marinade while they are cooking, then turn them and cook for another couple of minutes. Serve with the aloo bhaji, salad leaves, and lemon or lime wedges.

PENNE PASTA

with broccoli and Parmesan

This seems a bit bizarre, I know, but do give it a go because it tastes sublime and has been known to convert ardent broccoli haters into fans. Do use good-quality fresh pasta, preferably made with egg, and definitely not the dried quick-cook variety, which has a horrid texture. Good pasta should work with the sauce and absorb just the right amount.

Serves 4

1½ lb (675 g) broccoli
12 oz–1 lb (350–450 g) fresh penne pasta
½ cup extra-virgin olive oil

2 large cloves garlic, crushed
1 tablespoon freshly squeezed lemon juice
½ cup finely grated Parmesan
Maldon or sea salt and freshly ground
    black pepper

Bring two large pans of well-salted water to a boil. Discard the large stalks from the broccoli and cut the green heads into small florets. You want to be left with about 1 lb (450 g). Add the broccoli to one pan, bring back to a boil, and cook for 2 minutes. Drain, reserving some of the cooking water and set aside half of the nicest-looking florets. Add the pasta to the second pan and cook for 6–8 minutes, or according to the package directions, until *al dente*. Meanwhile, heat half the oil in a large, deep skillet. Add the garlic and the other half of the broccoli florets and fry over a high heat for 2–3 minutes until the florets are lightly browned and quite soft. Tip them into a food processor and add the rest of the olive oil, 6 tablespoons of the reserved broccoli water, the lemon juice, half the Parmesan, and plenty of seasoning. Blitz the mixture for a minute or so until really smooth.

Drain the pasta well, return it to the pan with the broccoli sauce, and toss together well. Now add the reserved florets and toss lightly so that you don't break up the whole florets too much. Spoon into 4 warmed pasta bowls, sprinkle over the rest of the Parmesan, and serve.

SEARED MEDALLIONS OF SALMON

with hot pepper marmalade and crème fraîche raita

OK, I've stolen the idea for this from another chef, so apologies to Peter Gordon of the Sugar Club in London for basing this on his wonderful signature dish of scallops with chili jam and crème fraîche. But I've changed it a lot, he said in meek defense, and whatever, it's pretty damn good. Enough said!

Serves 4

sunflower oil for deep-frying, plus
   2 tablespoons
1 small bunch of fresh chives
12 oz (350 g) piece skinned salmon fillet,
   taken from a large fish
lemon juice
salt and freshly ground black pepper

For the hot pepper marmalade:
1 medium red onion, finely chopped
2 cloves garlic, finely chopped
1 teaspoon ground coriander
2 tablespoons olive oil
2 red bell peppers, seeded and cut into strips

1 inch (2.5 cm) piece fresh ginger root,
   peeled and finely grated
1 long, thin red chili pepper, finely chopped
   (seeds and all)
Scant ½ cup red wine vinegar (preferably
   Cabernet Sauvignon)
3½ tablespoons soft light brown sugar

For the crème fraîche raita:
4 tablespoons crème fraîche or sour cream
2 inch (5 cm) piece cucumber, peeled,
   seeded and diced
1 small cooked potato, finely diced
Tomatoes Concassées (see page 184),
   use 2 tomatoes
2 tablespoons chopped fresh cilantro

For the hot pepper marmalade, sweat the onion, garlic, and ground coriander in the oil for about 5 minutes until soft and lightly browned. Add the red peppers, ginger, and chili and cook over a low heat for another 10 minutes until soft. Add the vinegar and the sugar, bring up to a simmer and leave to cook gently for 20 minutes, giving the mixture a stir every now and then.

For the raita, mix all the ingredients together, cover and chill in the refrigerator until needed.

Pour about ½ inch (1 cm) oil into a small pan and heat to 325°F (160°C). Chop the chives into 3 inch (7.5 cm) lengths, then deep-fry them for 15–20 seconds. Drain on paper towels. Cut the salmon fillet in half down the natural central seam and then slice each piece across into about 6 thin medallions. Heat a large skillet until very hot. Add 2 tablespoons oil, then flash-fry the salmon for about 2 minutes on one side only. Quickly lift the slices onto a baking sheet and season with a little lemon juice, salt and pepper.

Spoon some hot pepper marmalade onto each plate, then arrange 3 pieces of the salmon around it. Add a spoonful of the raita, pile the deep-fried chives on top, and serve.

FETA FRITTATA

with smoked salmon and herbed crème fraîche

This is really just a nice, big, thick wedge of omelet with lots of tasty bits in it – traditional Italian stuff. The Italians could teach us a thing or two about cooking and eating, and drinking come to think of it, not to mention how to have a good time! You could alternatively cook this in a deep skillet on the stove top and brown off the top under the broiler, but the finished frittata will not be quite so thick.

Serves 8

1 tablespoon olive oil
1 bunch of green onions, trimmed and sliced
2 oz (50 g) arugula
8 medium farm-fresh eggs
Scant 1 cup crème fraîche
2 tablespoons chopped fresh flat-leaf parsley

2 Roasted Red Bell Peppers (see page 185), cut into long, thin strips
4 oz (100 g) feta cheese, crumbled
Maldon or sea salt and freshly ground white pepper
1 tablespoon each chopped fresh dill, mint, and parsley
10 oz (275 g) Scottish smoked salmon

Preheat the oven to 325°F (160°C). Grease and line the bottom of an 8 inch (20 cm) clip-sided cake pan with nonstick baking parchment, taking the paper over the join and very slightly up the sides just in case your pan is not watertight.

Heat the oil in a pan. Add the green onions and fry over a high heat for about 2 minutes until soft and lightly tinged with brown. Add the arugula and stir it around in the hot pan until it has only just wilted, then take the pan off the heat.

Break the eggs into a bowl and whisk in 3 tablespoons of the crème fraîche. Stir in the chopped parsley, roasted red peppers, feta cheese, and the green onion and arugula mix. Season well with salt and pepper.

Pour the mixture into the cake pan and bake in the oven for 40–45 minutes until just set. Remove and leave to cool to room temperature.

Mix the remaining crème fraîche with the chopped herbs and some seasoning to taste. Slice the frittata into 8 slices and place one on each plate. Loosely pile some smoked salmon alongside and serve with a spoonful of the herbed crème fraîche.

PRESSED TERRINE OF POTATO, CHICKEN LIVERS, AND PROSCIUTTO

This was a bit of a culinary triumph – the idea had been floating around in my head since I tasted a potato and *foie gras* terrine at some posh French noshery years ago. This version uses cheap ingredients (except for the prosciutto) and is, I have to say in all modesty, pretty damn good. Ideal for a big dinner-party first course with all the work done in advance, or for a slightly smaller number at lunch time. If you have trouble slicing it, try using an electric knife – they have to be useful for something!

Serves 12

2 (8 oz) (225 g) firm main-crop potatoes
8 thin slices prosciutto
¾ cup butter
2 cloves garlic, finely chopped
3 tablespoons chopped fresh flat-leaf parsley
Maldon or sea salt and freshly ground
   white pepper

2 tablespoons sunflower oil
1½ lb (675 g) fresh chicken livers, trimmed
¼ cup finely grated Parmesan

To serve:
4 tablespoons Herb Oil (see page 186)
3 oz (75 g) mixed baby salad leaves

You will need to prepare this terrine the day before you want to serve it as it has to be pressed overnight. First thing in the morning, boil the whole, unpeeled potatoes in salted water for 30–40 minutes until tender when pierced with a skewer. Drain them, leave to go cold and then chill them in the refrigerator for quite a few hours, during which time they will firm up and become much easier to slice. (If you can do this the night before, even better.)

Lightly oil a 3 inch (7.5 cm) deep, 3 × 10 inch (7.5 × 25 cm) terrine dish (a Le Creuset terrine is ideal) and then line it with some plastic wrap so that the edges are left overhanging. Now line the dish with the slices of prosciutto, overlapping them slightly and leaving about 3 inches (7.5 cm) overhanging all the way round.

Peel the potatoes and cut each one across into ¼ inch (5 mm) thick slices. Melt the butter with the garlic in a small pan and leave it to cook over a very gentle heat for 10 minutes. Stir in the chopped parsley and plenty of seasoning and set it aside to cool but not set.

Heat half the oil in a large, nonstick skillet. Add half the chicken livers and fry them over a high heat, turning them now and then, for about 2–3 minutes until nicely browned but still rare and juicy in the center. Season well with salt and pepper and set aside while you cook the rest.

To assemble the terrine, pour a thin layer of the garlic butter into the dish and tilt it back and forth until it has completely covered the bottom. Now layer one-third of the potato slices over the butter and season them well with salt and pepper. Cover the potatoes with half the chicken livers and sprinkle them with half of the Parmesan. Spoon over some more of the garlic butter and repeat these layers once more, remembering to season them as you go. Now cover the top of the terrine with the remaining one-third of the sliced potatoes and then fold the overhanging edges of the Parma ham over the top so that the potatoes are completely covered. Fold over the plastic wrap – if there isn't quite enough, cover with another sheet – and then weigh down the terrine. You can do this either by placing a second terrine on top and filling it with heavy objects, or by cutting a piece of card to fit inside the top edge, covering the terrine dish in aluminum foil and then weighing it down with metal weights or a few unopened cans. Slide it into the refrigerator and leave it to chill overnight.

To serve, gently toss the prepared salad leaves with some of the herb oil. Fold the plastic wrap back from the top of the terrine and invert it onto a board or serving dish. Using a very sharp knife, carve it into 12 thin slices and place them on the plates. Pile the dressed salad leaves alongside, drizzle around the remaining herb oil, and serve, perhaps with some crusty French bread.

SALT AND PEPPER SQUID

with stir-fried vegetables

I'm not quite sure why, but dry-frying salt and pepper together produces a really wonderful aromatic flavor that's more than just salt and pepper. Don't overcrowd the pan when deep-frying or the pieces will stick together, and by the time the rings are golden, the squid will be overcooked and rubbery. Now I know that I don't really have to say this, but I'm going to. Don't use frozen squid – but of course, you wouldn't! It would be quite in order to serve wedges of lemon to squeeze over the squid.

Serves 4

8 oz (225 g) cleaned squid
1½ teaspoons Maldon or sea salt
2 teaspoons Szechwan peppercorns
sunflower oil, for deep-frying
2 tablespoons self-rising flour

For the stir-fried vegetables:
2 oz (50 g) snow peas
2 oz (50 g) piece red bell pepper

2 tablespoons sunflower oil
2 green onions, chopped
1 teaspoon finely chopped ginger root
1 teaspoon finely chopped garlic
2 oz (50 g) fresh bean sprouts
2 teaspoons Thai fish sauce
2 teaspoons lime juice
1 tablespoon chopped fresh cilantro

Slice the squid across into thin rings and separate the tentacles if large. Heat a dry, heavy-bottomed skillet over a medium heat. Add the salt and stir it around for a couple of minutes until it begins to look a bit gray. Tip it into a bowl, reheat the pan, then add the Szechwan peppercorns and toss them around until they darken slightly and start to smell aromatic. Grind the salt and peppercorns to a fine powder in a coffee grinder or a mortar and pestle.

Pour some oil into a large pan so that it is about one-third full and heat it to 375°F (190°C). Mix the salt and pepper powder with the flour, place it in a plastic bag and add the squid. Give the bag a good shake so that all the pieces of squid become evenly coated in the highly seasoned flour Deep-fry 5–6 pieces at a time in the hot oil for just 30–45 seconds until crisp and golden. Lift out with a slotted spoon onto a paper-lined baking sheet and keep warm in a low oven.

For the stir-fried vegetables, cut the snow peas and the piece of red pepper into strips about the same thickness as the bean sprouts. Heat a large, deep skillet or wok until very hot. Add the oil, green onion, ginger, and garlic, and stir around for a few seconds. Then throw in the snow peas and red pepper and stir-fry for 1 minute. Take the pan off the heat and stir in the bean sprouts, fish sauce, lime juice, and cilantro.

Pile the salt and pepper squid slightly to one side of 4 warmed plates, pile a little of the stir-fried vegetables alongside and serve.

Omelets

The secret of a good omelet is in ingredients with impeccable credentials, and this means farm eggs — but the real hand-gathered ones from the farmyard. Once you've cooked them and seen the difference in the color (yes, a real yellow omelet), never mind the taste, you'll be converted.

MULL CHEDDAR OMELET

with parsley

A simple dish which is a real star. The cheese must be properly matured, unpasteurized Cheddar from a good cheese-maker. Mull Cheddar is probably the best you can get, but there are some other crackers around. Taste this and you'll realize that simple is best.

Serves 1

2 medium farm-fresh eggs
1 tablespoon heavy cream
Maldon or sea salt and freshly ground
   white pepper

1 tablespoon oil or melted butter
¼ cup coarsely grated Mull Cheddar or sharp
   Cheddar cheese
1 teaspoon chopped fresh parsley

Break the eggs into a bowl. Add the cream and season with a little salt and pepper. Lightly whisk together with a fork until the whites and yolks are only just combined.

Heat an 8 inch (20 cm) skillet over a low–medium heat. Add the oil or butter and, as soon as it is hot, pour in the eggs and swirl them around a bit so that they coat the bottom of the pan. As soon as they begin to set over the bottom, stir them into the center of the pan with the back of a fork so that the runny egg can move about and come into contact with the hot pan.

As soon as the omelet mixture stops moving about (but is still very moist on top), sprinkle over the grated cheese and the chopped parsley and leave for just a few seconds. Lift the pan off the heat, tilt it toward you at an angle of 45 degrees, and, using a fork, release the farthermost edge of the omelet and roll it over toward the lower edge of the pan nearest you. Cover the pan with a plate, then turn the two over together so that the omelet is now on the plate, and eat straightaway.

CHANTERELLE MUSHROOM OMELET

with garlic and chives

Chanterelles have a very distinctive, apricoty flavor and are one of my favorite mushrooms, available from the end of July through mid-October. They are at their best, and cheapest, in September and, being one of the most perfumed of mushrooms, they're great in omelets. Using other varieties of mushroom will give good results but they won't be in the same league as the chanterelle.

Serves 1

1 tablespoon oil or melted butter
1 small clove garlic, finely chopped
4 oz (100 g) chanterelle mushrooms,
    wiped clean, halved if large
Maldon or sea salt and freshly ground
    white pepper

2 medium farm-fresh eggs
1 tablespoon heavy cream
1 tablespoon butter
1 small bunch of fresh chives,
    roughly chopped

Heat the oil or melted butter in a skillet. Add the garlic and cook for a few seconds before throwing in the mushrooms. Stir-fry over a high heat for about a minute until just cooked through. Season with salt and pepper.

Break the eggs into a bowl, add the cream, and season with a little salt and pepper. Lightly whisk together with a fork until the whites and yolks are only just combined.

Heat an 8 inch (20 cm) skillet over a low–medium heat. Add the butter and, as soon as it is hot, pour in the eggs and swirl them around a bit so that they coat the bottom of the pan. As soon as they begin to set over the bottom, start stirring them into the center of the pan with the back of a fork so that the runny egg can move about and come into contact with the hot pan.

As soon as the omelet mixture stops moving about (but is still very moist on top), sprinkle over the mushrooms, garlic, and chopped chives, and leave for just a few seconds. Lift the pan off the heat, tilt it toward you at an angle of 45 degrees, and, using a fork, release the farthermost edge of the omelet and roll it over toward the lower edge of the pan nearest you. Cover the pan with a plate, then turn the two over together so that the omelet is now on the plate, and eat straightaway.

SMOKED HADDOCK, PUY LENTIL, AND TARRAGON OMELET

This variation adds smoky haddock, earthy lentils, and aromatic tarragon for a taste sensation. I cooked this omelet in a challenge to find the best omelet in Scotland and was up against chefs who used *foie gras*, truffles, and fancy sauces with theirs. Suffice to say that simplicity won the day! Cook a pile of lentils as they keep in the refrigerator for a couple of days and even freeze well.

Serves 1

2 medium farm-fresh eggs

1 tablespoon heavy cream

Maldon or sea salt and freshly ground
   white pepper

1 tablespoon oil or melted butter

½ – ¾ cooked, flaked smoked haddock

1 teaspoon chopped fresh tarragon

For the lentils:

1¼ cups green Puy lentils

1 halved head of garlic

1 fresh bay leaf

1 sprig of fresh thyme

1 carrot, peeled and roughly chopped

Put the lentils in a pan with 3 times the amount of water, the garlic, bay leaf, thyme, carrot, and a pinch of salt. Simmer for 15–20 minutes, or until you can crush a lentil between finger and thumb. Take care not to overcook them. Drain, discard the garlic, bay leaf, thyme, and carrot, and set aside.

Break the eggs into a bowl. Add the cream and season with a little salt and pepper. Lightly whisk together with a fork until the whites and yolks are only just combined.

Heat an 8 inch (20 cm) skillet over a low–medium heat. Add the oil or butter and, as soon as it is hot, pour in the eggs and swirl them around a bit so that they coat the bottom of the pan. As soon as they begin to set over the bottom, start stirring them into the center of the pan with the back of a fork so that the runny egg can move about and come into contact with the hot bottom.

As soon as the omelet mixture stops moving about (but is still very moist on top), sprinkle over the flaked haddock, a couple of tablespoons of the lentils, and the chopped tarragon, and leave for just a few seconds. Lift the pan off the heat, tilt it toward you at an angle of 45 degrees, and, using a fork, release the farthermost edge of the omelet and roll it over toward the lower edge of the pan nearest you. Cover the pan with a plate, then turn the two over together so that the omelet is now on the plate, and eat straightaway.

THAI CRAB OMELET

with green onions and ginger

You might have guessed by now that I'm well into my Thai flavorings, so I thought I would try them in an omelet, and I was chuffed with the results. Obviously fresh crabmeat is best, but frozen or pasteurized would do here as its flavor has strong support from the spices.

Serves 1

¼ cup Chicken Stock (see page 181)
¾ teaspoon Thai fish sauce or dark soy sauce
½ teaspoon soft light brown sugar
¼ teaspoon sesame oil
2 medium farm-fresh eggs
Maldon or sea salt and freshly ground
   white pepper

4 teaspoons sunflower oil
½ teaspoon freshly grated ginger root
1 oz (25 g) snow peas, thinly shredded
1 oz (25 g) fresh bean sprouts
1 green onion, halved and cut into
   very fine shreds
½ cup fresh white crabmeat
1 tablespoon chopped fresh cilantro

Put the chicken stock, ½ teaspoon of the fish sauce or dark soy sauce, a pinch of the sugar, and the sesame oil into a small pan. Bring up to a boil and simmer very gently for 1 minute. Keep hot over a very low heat.

Break the eggs into a bowl, add the rest of the fish sauce or soy sauce, the sugar, and some salt and pepper, and beat together until just mixed. Set aside.

Heat 1 teaspoon of the sunflower oil in a small saucepan over a high heat. Add the ginger and snow peas and stir-fry for 1 minute. Remove from the heat and stir in the bean sprouts and the green onion shreds. Bring back to the heat and add the eggs to the pan. Swirl them around a bit so that they coat the bottom of the pan. As soon as they begin to set over the bottom, start stirring them into the center of the pan with the back of a fork so that the runny egg can move about and come into contact with the hot bottom.

As soon as the omelet mixture stops moving about (but is still very moist on top), sprinkle over the crabmeat and the chopped cilantro and leave for just a few seconds. Lift the pan off the heat, tilt it toward you at an angle of 45 degrees, and, using a fork, release the farthermost edge of the omelet and roll it over toward the lower edge of the pan nearest you. Cover the pan with a plate, and then turn the two over together so that the omelet is now on the plate. Pour over the sauce and eat straightaway.

Scottish Oatcakes

These oatcakes are traditionally cooked on a griddle over an open fire, but you can get a great result by baking them in the oven too. They can be made well in advance, cooled and stored in an airtight container. When made, a nice bit of cheese is all you really need, but use your imagination and the sky is the limit – as the following four recipes demonstrate.

SCOTTISH OATCAKES

with goat cheese, cherry tomatoes, and basil

The lovely, soft, creamy texture of goat cheese is the perfect foil for the sharp sweetness of cherry tomatoes and basil.

Serves 4

1½ cups medium oatmeal, plus extra
   for dusting
¼ teaspoon baking soda
½ teaspoon salt
1 tablespoon bacon fat, lard, or butter
⅔ cup water

2 tablespoon butter, melted
6 oz (75 g) crumbled goat cheese
24 cherry plum tomatoes, halved
1–2 tablespoons extra-virgin olive oil
Maldon or sea salt and freshly ground
   black pepper
8 sprigs of fresh basil

Preheat the oven to 350°F (180°C). Put the oatmeal, baking of soda, and salt into a bowl and mix well. Place the fat, lard, or butter and water in a small pan and heat until the fat has melted. Make a well in the center of the oatmeal, add the liquid and mix together with a spatula. The mixture will initially seem a bit wet but the oatmeal will gradually absorb all the liquid to give you a soft dough. Divide the mixture into 2 and roll each piece out on a work surface lightly dusted with oatmeal to a 6 inch (15 cm) round about ¼ inch (5 mm) thick. Don't worry if the edges aren't very neat – they look better that way. Cut into quarters (farls, as they say in Scotland), brush off the excess oatmeal, and place on an ungreased baking sheet. Bake for about 20 minutes, turning the oatcakes every 5 minutes or so to stop them from steaming and going stodgy, until crisp and lightly golden. Leave to cool on a wire rack.

To serve, brush the oatcakes with some melted butter and place 2 pieces on each serving plate. Pile the goat cheese and cherry tomatoes on top, drizzle with a little olive oil, and then sprinkle with a little salt and pepper. Garnish with the sprigs of fresh basil.

SCOTTISH OATCAKES

with chicken livers, red onion conserve, and arugula

These are a bit messy for finger eating but are good enough for the proper knife and fork treatment. One makes a great starter, two, a smashing lunch, three and you're a pig, but I bet you smile a lot! There will be more red onion conserve than you need, so spoon the rest into a jar, pour a thin layer of oil on top, and store it in the refrigerator. It will keep for 6–8 weeks and goes really well with all sorts of hot and cold meats, or cheese.

Serves 4

2 tablespoons butter

12 oz (350 g) chicken livers, trimmed

Maldon salt or sea salt and freshly ground
    black pepper

1 quantity Scottish Oatcakes (see page 60)

½ cup arugula leaves

a few drops of olive oil and freshly squeezed
    lemon juice

For the red onion conserve
    (makes about 1 lb) (450 g):

5 tablespoons olive oil

3¼ lb (1.5 kg) red onions, thinly sliced

½ cup sherry vinegar or Cabernet Sauvignon
    vinegar

2 tablespoons crème de cassis (optional)

For the red onion conserve, heat the oil in a large, heavy-bottomed pan. Add the onions and cook over a low–medium heat, stirring now and then, for 1 hour until the onions are very soft and richly caramelized. Add the vinegar and simmer for another 10 minutes until the harsh flavor of the vinegar has been boiled off and the conserve has thickened. Stir in the crème de cassis, if using, season to taste with salt and pepper, and keep warm over a low heat.

Heat the butter in a large skillet. Add the chicken livers and fry over a high heat, turning them as they brown, for about 3 minutes until they are nicely browned on the outside but still pink and juicy in the center. Season with salt and pepper and then arrange over the top of each oatcake. Spoon a little of the warmed onion conserve in among the livers. Toss the arugula leaves with the oil and lemon juice and season to taste with salt and pepper. Pile on top of each oatcake and serve.

SCOTTISH OATCAKES

with blue cheese, walnuts, and watercress

There are some cracking Scottish blue cheeses, such as Lanark Blue and Dunsyre Blue, but Bleu de Bresse, Shropshire Blue, or Stilton would be just as satisfying.

Serves 4

6 oz (175 g) blue cheese
1 recipe Scottish Oatcakes (see page 60)
½ cup walnut pieces

8–10 sprigs of watercress, large stalks
   removed
a few drops of extra-virgin olive oil
Maldon or sea salt and freshly ground
   black pepper

Break the cheese into small crumbly pieces and divide it between the oatcakes, with the walnut pieces. Toss the watercress leaves with a little oil and a little seasoning. Arrange the oatcakes on a baking sheet and slide them under a hot broiler for about 1 minute until the cheese just begins to melt. Quickly transfer them to serving plates, pile the watercress on top, and serve.

SCOTTISH OATCAKES

with creamy scrambled eggs and smoked salmon

This would also make great breakfast material, again down the knife and fork route. Serve with a compote of fruit and a glass of freshly squeezed orange juice to someone you love.

Serves 4

6 farm-fresh eggs
Maldon or sea salt and freshly ground
   black pepper
2 tablespoons butter

4 tablespoons heavy cream (optional)
1 recipe Scottish Oatcakes (see page 60)
2–3 oz (50–75 g) thinly sliced Scottish
   smoked salmon
chopped fresh chives, to garnish

Break the eggs into a bowl, season and beat together lightly with a fork. Melt half the butter in a small nonstick pan. Swirl it around so that it coats the sides a little. Add the eggs and cook over a medium heat, stirring all the time, for about 2 minutes or until the eggs are half-set. Take off the heat, add the rest of the butter, and the cream if using, and keep stirring, returning the pan to the heat briefly if necessary, until the eggs are soft and creamy. Spoon the scrambled eggs onto each oatcake and loosely pile the smoked salmon on top. Sprinkle with a few chopped chives and serve.

BAKED GOAT CHEESE IN PHYLLO PASTRY

with leeks and a tomato and mint sauce *vierge*

I've recently rediscovered phyllo in my cooking. It was quite a thing in the 1980s and got over-used, but sometimes I find it useful to delve back into the past and take the best bits of old dishes and rework them. Here you need good, ripe goat cheese – there are now some cracking Scottish ones around – and thin, firm leeks. You can make up the packages in advance and finish cooking them just before serving. The mint in the sauce works just a treat!

Serves 4

6 tablespons butter

8 oz (225 g) leeks, cleaned and sliced

4 tablespoons heavy cream or crème fraîche

Maldon or sea salt and freshly ground
   black pepper

6 sheets of phyllo pastry

4 (1½ oz) (40 g) slices goat cheese or
   2 (4 oz) (100 g) goat cheeses, halved into
   2 smaller discs

For the tomato and mint sauce *vierge*:

5 tablespoons olive oil

1 tablespoon white wine vinegar

Tomato Concassée (see page 184), use
   1 tomato

½ small red onion, very finely chopped

¼ teaspoon Maldon or sea salt and some
   freshly ground black pepper

1 tablespoon chopped fresh mint

Melt 2 tablespoons of the butter in a pan. Add the leeks and cook over a medium heat for about 3 minutes until they are just soft. Take the pan off the heat and stir in the cream or crème fraîche and plenty of seasoning. Cool slightly. Preheat the oven to 425°F (220°C).

Meanwhile, melt the remaining butter. Lay one sheet of phyllo pastry on a work surface and brush with some of the melted butter. Cover with another sheet of pastry, brush with more butter, and then cover with a third sheet. Set aside and repeat with the rest of the pastry. Now cut two 8 inch (20 cm) discs from each stack of pastry and place one piece of cheese in the center of each one. Spoon a quarter of the leeks on top of each piece of cheese and then, working around the edge of the pastry, pleat and fold it neatly over the top, sealing as you go with a little water. Brush each pakage all over with more butter and place on a lightly buttered baking sheet. Bake in the oven for 10–12 minutes until crisp and golden.

For the sauce *vierge*, put the oil, vinegar, tomatoes, red onion, salt and pepper into a small pan and let them just warm through over a very gentle heat. Stir in the mint. Place a phyllo package in the center of each plate and spoon some of the sauce around each package.

POTATO SCONES

topped with steam-fried eggs

Basic but brilliant. Use farm-fresh eggs and serve with maybe a slice or two of bacon on the side. The fried-egg trick is stolen from the rather clever Paul Rankin and has revolutionized fried-egg-making for me. The "long-haired" one also has one of Britain's best restaurants, Roscoff's in Belfast, which serves mighty fine scoff.

Serves 4

½ cup butter
8 farm-fresh eggs
4 teaspoons water

For the potato scones:

8 oz (225 g) floury main-crop potatoes
¼ cup butter
Maldon or sea salt and freshly ground
    black pepper
½ cup all-purpose flour

For the scones, peel the potatoes, cut them into chunks, and cook them in boiling salted water for 20 minutes or until tender. Drain them well, return them to the pan, and then toss them around over the heat for a few minutes to drive off all the excess moisture. Now either pass them through a potato ricer, or mash and then press through a sieve into a bowl. Beat in the butter and a pinch of salt and then work in the flour to make a soft dough. Turn the mixture out onto a lightly floured board, divide into 2, and knead once or twice until smooth. Roll out each piece into a round about ¼ inch (5 mm) thick and then cut each round into quarters. Prick well with a fork.

Heat a cast-iron griddle over a medium–high heat and lightly grease with a little butter. Lift on 4 of the scones and cook for 3 minutes on each side until golden brown and firm. Wrap in a dish towel to keep them warm while you cook the rest.

For the eggs, melt half the butter in a large skillet with a tight-fitting lid. Break in 4 of the eggs, trying to make sure they don't touch, and leave them until the whites have set. Then add 2 teaspoons of the water, put on the lid and leave for 45 seconds to 1 minute, during which time the water will turn to steam and lightly cook the tops of the eggs. Lift out, keep warm and repeat with the rest of the eggs.

Place a couple of the scones on each plate and spread with a little extra butter if you wish. Lift an egg onto each, season with some salt and freshly ground black pepper, and serve.

Vast areas of Scotland's staggeringly

beautiful countryside are not only

unpolluted, but unpopulated,

allowing a proliferation of furred

and feathered game, which provides

meat of an unrivaled quality.

MAIN COURSES

FISH

POACHED SEA TROUT

with herb mayonnaise, onion "grass" and gaufrette potatoes

Sea trout has a more delicate flavor than salmon and, as far as I know, nobody has managed to farm it yet, so it's bound to be wild. That is why I've chosen to poach it – not a cooking technique I use a lot – but, if done carefully, you get lovely moist fish with all its flavor intact. And what better to go with poached fish than a mayonnaise flavored with herbs? The onion "grass" is very easy and adds texture, as do the gaufrette potatoes which are just posh chips really.

Serves 6

3 (1½ lb) (675 g) sea trout
sunflower oil for deep-frying
4 fist-sized firm potatoes
1 medium onion
3 tablespoons all-purpose flour
Maldon or sea salt and freshly ground
   white pepper

For the court bouillon:
7½ cups water
½ lemon, sliced
1 fresh bay leaf
20 peppercorns
a handful of fresh parsley and tarragon stalks

For the herb mayonnaise:
1 medium farm-fresh egg yolk
1 teaspoon Dijon mustard
1 cup Herb Oil (see page 186)

For the salad garnish:
4 oz (100 g) mixed baby salad leaves,
   such as arugula, romaine, and fennel herb
a few drops of olive oil
a few drops of lemon juice

Fillet the sea trout, taking care to use short, gentle strokes because the flesh is quite soft, then skin them. Lay each fillet skinned-side up and, starting at the wider head end, roll each one up into a coil. Secure it at the tail end by pushing a wooden toothpick right through into the center. Stand each one upright so that it looks like a tower with a rose-shaped top and set to one side.

    Put all the ingredients for the court bouillon in a small roasting pan. Bring up to a rapid simmer and keep hot over a low heat.

For the herb mayonnaise, mix the egg yolk and mustard together in a bowl and then very gradually whisk in the herb oil until the finished mixture is thick and silky smooth. Cover with some plastic wrap and chill until needed.

Pour some of the sunflower oil into a large pan and heat to 350°F (180°C). Meanwhile, cut each potato across into 2 shorter halves and then thinly slice on a mandolin fitted with a ridged blade. With every slice, give the potato a 90-degree turn so that the slices take on a lattice design. Dry them well on paper towels and deep-fry a handful at a time until crisp and golden. Lift out with a slotted spoon onto a wax paper-lined baking sheet and keep warm in a low oven. To make the onion "grass," cut the onion in half and thinly slice on the mandolin. Separate the strands into a bowl, add the flour and some salt and pepper, and work everything together with your fingertips so that all the pieces get well coated in the flour. Deep-fry a handful at a time until crisp and golden and keep warm alongside the potatoes.

Bring the court bouillon back up to a simmer. Add the sea trout rolls still in an upright position and poach them for just 6 minutes. While they are cooking, toss the salad leaves with a little oil, lemon juice, and some seasoning until they glisten like wet skin.

Lift the sea trout out of the pan, let the excess liquid drain away, and then set slightly to one side of each serving plate. Pile the onion "grass" on top of each piece of salmon, pile some of the potatoes and salad alongside, and garnish with 2 small ovals of the herb mayonnaise.

ROAST MONKFISH

with cumin-roasted carrots and a spicy carrot juice sauce

Sauces made with vegetable juices are all the rage at the moment and deservedly so. Store-bought carrot juice is fine (you'll find it in health food stores) but if you have a juicer try out beet, asparagus, red bell pepper and celery too. In this dish the sauce is finished with butter but you could use olive oil instead, which doesn't emulsify like the butter but gives the finished sauce a nice speckled effect.

Serves 4

1½ lb (675 g) large monkfish fillets
Maldon or sea salt and freshly ground white
    pepper
sunflower oil
16 sprigs of fresh cilantro

For the cumin-roasted carrots:

1 lb (450 g) medium-sized carrots, peeled
1 tablespoon sunflower oil
2 teaspoons ground cumin

For the spicy carrot juice sauce:

1 teaspoon yellow mustard seeds
1 teaspoon cumin seeds
1 teaspoon coriander seeds
2 teaspoons sunflower oil
½ inch (1 cm) piece fresh ginger root, peeled
    and chopped
1¼ cups fresh carrot juice
    (homemade or store-bought)
1¼ cups Chicken Stock
    (see page 181)
¼ cup unsalted butter
1 tablespoon chopped fresh cilantro

For the sauce, heat a dry, heavy-bottomed pan over a high heat. Add the yellow mustard seeds and fry for a few seconds until they begin to pop. Tip them into a small bowl and set aside. Add the cumin and coriander seeds to the dry pan and fry until they have darkened very slightly and are starting to smell aromatic. Tip them into a second bowl and set aside. Heat the oil in a medium-size pan. Add the ginger and fry for a couple of minutes until lightly golden. Add the roasted cumin and coriander seeds and fry for another minute. Add the carrot juice and stock, bring to a boil, and boil rapidly until reduced by about three-quarters. Remove from the heat and set aside.

For the cumin-roasted carrots, preheat the oven to 425°F (220°C). Cut each carrot in half into 2 shorter pieces and then cut each piece in half lengthwise. Drop into a pan of boiling salted water and cook for 2–3 minutes. Drain and refresh under running cold water. Dry well on paper towels. Transfer the carrots to a small roasting pan and add the oil, ground cumin, and some salt and pepper. Toss together so the carrots get evenly coated in the spices and then slide the pan into the oven for 20–30 minutes, or until the carrots are cooked to your liking. I like them with a little hint of crunch inside.

Meanwhile, cut the monkfish into twelve ¾ inch (2 cm) slices and flatten slightly with the palm of your hand into discs. Heat a heavy-bottomed skillet over a high heat. Season the monkfish with some salt and pepper. As soon as the pan is hot, brush it with a little oil, add 2 or 3 pieces of monkfish, and cook them for 2 minutes on the first side, then 1 minute on the second side, until just cooked through. Lift them onto a plate, cover with some aluminum foil, and repeat with the rest of the slices. Leave to relax somewhere warm for a few minutes.

Strain the carrot juice sauce through a fine sieve into a clean pan and bring it back to a boil. Lower the heat and then whisk in the butter, a little piece at a time, to make a smooth, glossy sauce. Stir in the roasted yellow mustard seeds and chopped fresh cilantro and season to taste with a little salt and pepper.

Place a few of the carrots in the center of each plate and place a sprig of cilantro and a slice of the monkfish on top. Stack more carrots, cilantro sprigs, and monkfish until you have used 3 slices of fish per person, finishing with the carrots. Pour some of the sauce around the edge of the plate, garnish with the remaining sprigs of fresh cilantro, and serve.

SPICY SALMON

with a chilled cucumber salad

This dish started out as a Cajun Salmon but I changed the original spices after mixing up this recipe with another during a cookery show. And I'm very glad it happened too, because this is better than the original. The salmon is pretty spicy and I like some chili in the cucumber salad as well. However, if you are not a big chili fan, leave it out of the salad but not the salmon.

Serves 6

6 (6 oz) (175 g) pieces thick salmon fillet,
    unskinned
1 tablespoon paprika powder
1 teaspoon dried chili flakes
½ teaspoon dried thyme
½ teaspoon dried oregano
1 teaspoon black peppercorns
½ teaspoon cumin seeds

2 teaspoons Maldon or sea salt, plus extra
    for sprinkling
3 tablespoons olive oil, plus extra to serve

For the chilled cucumber salad:

2 cucumbers
1 large clove garlic, very finely chopped
1 tablespoon lemon or lime juice
1 long, thin red chili pepper, seeded and
    finely chopped
2 tablespoons chopped fresh cilantro

Score the skin of the salmon and set to one side. Put the paprika, chili flakes, thyme, oregano, black peppercorns, cumin seeds, and 2 teaspoons of salt into a mortar or coffee grinder and grind to a fine powder. Sprinkle over the bottom of a large plate. Brush the skin of the salmon with some of the olive oil and then dip only the skin side into the salt and spices, making sure that each piece gets coated in an even layer.

For the chilled cucumber salad, peel the cucumbers, cut them in half, and scoop out the seeds with a melon-baller or a teaspoon. Cut them lengthwise into long, thin shreds by hand, by using a Japanese vegetable turner or on the widest grating attachment of a mandolin and then dry well in a dish towel. Set aside in the refrigerator to chill until needed.

Heat a smooth, cast-iron griddle on the barbecue or on the stove top. Add a little olive oil and then the salmon, skin-side down. Cook over a medium heat for about 5 minutes until the skin is nice and crisp. Brush the flesh of the salmon pieces with the remaining oil, turn the fish over, and cook for another 2–3 minutes, until just cooked through. Lift the salmon pieces onto a baking sheet straightaway so that it doesn't continue to cook.

Add the garlic, lemon or lime juice, chili, cilantro, and a pinch of salt to the cucumber and toss together well. Pile the salad in the center of each plate and place a piece of salmon on top. Drizzle around a little more olive oil and serve.

BAKED HAKE

with spinach, spaghetti of carrots, and shellfish cream

When I cooked this dish for the army boys on Benbecula, I was out to impress, so I used lots of different shellfish in the sauce. Very tasty and "very cheffy." I would suggest that you stick to just one type – mussels would be my choice and you'll need about 3 lb (1.5 kg). The spaghetti of carrots can be cooked in advance and reheated, as can the sauce, but this is still a dish that requires quite a bit of culinary juggling. Hake is a personal favorite of mine, but a bit scarce. Cod works as an alternative.

Serves 6

¼ cup butter
6 (6 oz) (175 g) hake or cod fillets, skinned
juice of ½ lemon
Maldon or sea salt and freshly ground black
  pepper
2 cups dry white wine
2 tablespoons olive oil
1 clove garlic, crushed
2 lb (900 g) fresh spinach, washed and any
  large stalks removed
a small piece of butter

For the spaghetti of carrots:
6 oz (175 g) carrots, peeled
2 tablespoons butter
1 tablespoon lemon juice

For the shellfish cream sauce:
1 lb (450 g) fresh mussels
1 lb (450 g) razor shell clams
1 lb (450 g) cockles or small (Manilla) clams
6 oz (175 g) shelled scallops, cleaned
1¼ cups heavy cream
2–3 tablespoons chopped fresh chervil
a few drops of lemon juice

Heavily grease a shallow baking dish with some of the butter and place the hake fillets on top. Sprinkle them with the lemon juice, dot generously with the rest of the butter, and season with some salt and pepper. Pour over 6 tablespoons of the wine and set aside. Preheat the oven to 450°F (230°C).

Prepare the carrots by grating them into long, thin, spaghetti-like strands on a mandolin. If you don't have a mandolin, simply cut the carrots lengthwise into thin slices and then cut each slice lengthwise into very thin strands.

For the sauce, scrub all the shellfish and wash in plenty of cold water. Discard any that don't stay closed when given a sharp tap. Place the shellfish, one sort at a time, into a large pan with a splash more of the wine, cover and cook over a high heat. Allow 3–4 minutes for the mussels and razor shell clams and about 2 minutes for the Manilla clams. Discard any shellfish that remain closed. Pour the cooking liquor left in the pan into a clean pan, leaving behind the last couple of tablespoons, which might contain some sand. Bring back to a boil. Add the scallops, cover and poach them for 2–3 minutes until firm and just cooked. Lift the scallops onto a plate and pour the cooking liquor into a pitcher. When the shellfish are cool enough to handle, remove them from their shells and cut the scallops and razor shell clams into small, neat pieces.

Place 2 cups of the shellfish cooking liquid in a pan with the rest of the white wine and bring to a boil. Leave to boil vigorously until reduced to about 6 tablespoons. Add the heavy cream, bring it back to a boil, and leave to boil until it has reduced and thickened enough to coat the back of a wooden spoon. Keep the sauce warm over a very low heat.

Slide the hake fillets into the oven and bake them for 5–6 minutes until opaque and firm in the center. Meanwhile, melt the "spaghetti" butter in a pan. Add the carrots, lemon juice, and some seasoning, and cook over a medium heat, stirring until the carrots are just soft and covered in a rich, buttery glaze – about 10 minutes. Keep them warm.

Heat the olive oil in another large pan. Add the garlic and spinach, and cook, stirring, until the spinach has wilted. Tip it into a colander and press out the excess liquid; then transfer it to a cutting board and roughly chop it. Return it to the pan with a small piece of butter and some salt and pepper, and toss together over a low heat for a few seconds. Stir the cooked shellfish into the cream sauce and let it warm through.

To serve, spoon the spinach into the centers of 4 warmed plates. Place a piece of fish on top of the spinach and then using a fork twist some of the carrots into a pile on top of each one. Stir the chopped chervil into the sauce and taste it for seasoning. Add a few drops of lemon juice and spoon some around the edges of the plates.

ROAST MONKFISH

with *salsa verde* chickpeas and deep-fried prosciutto

Chickpeas are tricky little beggars to cook – the older they are, the longer they take – but I would always advise erring on the side of overcooking as there are few things worse than undercooked chickpeas. The problem is easily solved by using precooked canned ones, not quite as tasty but much less of a fuss. When processing the *salsa verde*, be careful not to overwork it. You want a nice, chunky texture, not baby food. The *salsa verde* chickpeas and prosciutto can all be prepared in advance, leaving just the cooking of the monkfish to the last minute.

Serves 4

2 lb (900 g) monkfish fillets
sunflower oil for frying
4 thin slices prosciutto
a little Herb Oil (see page 186), to serve

For the *salsa verde* chickpeas:
2¼ cups dried chickpeas, soaked overnight
3–4 cloves garlic, peeled but left whole
4 small, fresh bay leaves

½ cup fresh flat-leaf parsley
¼ cup fresh basil leaves
¼ cup fresh mint leaves
2 cloves garlic, crushed
2 tablespoons salted capers, washed
1 (2 oz) (50 g) can anchovy fillets, drained
1 tablespoon red wine vinegar
3–4 tablespoons extra-virgin olive oil
1 teaspoon Dijon mustard
Maldon or sea salt and freshly ground
    black pepper

First prepare the chickpeas. Drain and place them in a pan with enough cold water to cover. Bring to a boil and cook vigorously for 10 minutes. Drain and rinse under cold water. Return them to the pan and cover with more water (boiling from the kettle will speed things up a little bit). Bring them back to a boil, add the whole garlic cloves and the bay leaves, and leave to simmer until tender. This can be anywhere from 1½ to 3 hours, depending on how old the chickpeas are.

Meanwhile, for the *salsa verde*, remove any large stalks from the parsley, basil, and mint and place the leaves in a food processor with the crushed garlic, capers, and anchovies. Blend everything together for a few seconds until smooth; then scrape the mixture into a bowl and gradually whisk in the vinegar and the oil. Stir in the mustard and season to taste with a little salt and some freshly ground pepper. Set aside.

Trim any membrane off the outside of the monkfish fillets and then cut them across into 8 equal size, neat chunks.

When the chickpeas are just about ready, pour ¾ inch (2 cm) sunflower oil into a medium-size pan and heat it to 350°F (180°C). Deep-fry the prosciutto, 2 slices at a time, for about 30 seconds, until nice and crisp. Drain on paper towels and set aside. Now heat a large, heavy-bottomed skillet until it is very hot. Add some oil and the monkfish pieces – don't overcrowd the pan (if your pan is not very large, do this in 2 batches). Fry over a high heat for about 4 minutes on each side until the pieces are nicely browned but only just cooked through in the center.

Drain the chickpeas well and discard the garlic cloves and the bay leaves. Return the chickpeas to the pan with the *salsa verde* and stir together over a low heat until they have just heated through; don't leave them over the heat for too long or the sauce will lose its lovely, bright green color. Spoon the chickpeas into the center of 4 warmed plates, arrange the pieces of monkfish on top, and garnish with the prosciutto. Drizzle a little herb oil around the mound on each plate and serve.

BAKED WHOLE TURBOT

with melted butter and new potatoes

While filming on a Barra trawler, one of the young fishermen, Ali McNeil, baked a turbot for me in the tiny ship's galley. He simply bunged it into a roasting pan and banged it in the oven for 40 minutes. No seasoning, butter, herbs, or lemon juice. I was expecting it to be dry and tasteless. He served me up a piece with potatoes and butter and it was a revelation – it was *so* tasty! It really hit home that when you've got top-quality ingredients, you don't need to do anything fancy. In the recipe I've added butter, seasoning, and lemon juice – just to get a bit more sauce – but the one thing you do need is a super-fresh turbot!

Serves 4

¼ cup butter
1 (3 lb) (1.5 kg) turbot, cleaned and gutted

juice of ½ lemon
Maldon or sea salt and freshly ground white pepper
1 lb (450 g) new potatoes, scrubbed

Preheat the oven to 350°F (180°C). Choose a large roasting pan which is big enough to accommodate the turbot and grease it generously with some of the butter. Cut the head off the fish, lay the turbot in the pan, and then dot the top of it with the rest of the butter. Pour over the lemon juice and season the fish with some salt and pepper. Slide the pan into the oven and leave the fish to roast, uncovered, for 30 minutes. Meanwhile, cook the potatoes in some boiling salted water for 20 minutes or until tender.

Remove the turbot from the oven, run a knife down its backbone, and transfer the top 2 fillets to serving plates. Lift off the bone and then put the remaining 2 fillets on the other 2 plates. Serve with the boiled new potatoes and the cooking juices poured over.

ROAST SALMON

with lobster vinaigrette and zucchini fritters

Lobster vinaigrette may seem a bit extravagant – and, well, in a way it is – but it makes one lobster go round four people and the flavor that it gives to the sauce is heaven.

The zucchini fritters can be made a few hours ahead and reheated in the oven, leaving you with the frying of the salmon and the assembly of the vinaigrette just prior to serving those lucky guests of yours.

Serves 4

sunflower oil
4 (5 oz) (150 g) pieces salmon fillet
lemon juice
Maldon or sea salt and freshly ground
   white pepper

For the lobster vinaigrette:
1 (1¼ lb) (550 g) cooked lobster
¼ cup olive oil
1 Roasted Red Bell Pepper (see page 185),
   diced
Tomatoes Concassées (see page 184),
   use 3 tomatoes

1 tablespoon chopped fresh cilantro
1 tablespoon chopped fresh basil
2 tablespoons balsamic vinegar

For the zucchini fritters:
3 medium zucchini, coarsely grated
1 teaspoon Maldon or sea salt, plus a good
   pinch for the egg whites
2 medium farm-fresh eggs, separated
⅔ cup whipping cream
⅔ cup all-purpose flour
2 green onions, finely chopped
sunflower oil for shallow-frying

For the lobster vinaigrette, remove the meat from the lobster claws and tail and cut it into ¼ inch (5 mm) dice. Set aside until you are ready to serve. Preheat the oven to 225°F (110°C).

For the zucchini fritters, mix the grated zucchini with the teaspoon of salt and leave to drain in a sieve for 15 minutes. Rinse off the salt, squeeze out the excess water, and dry well on paper towels. Whisk the egg yolks and cream together in a bowl and then whisk in the flour to make a smooth batter. Stir in the green onions and the zucchini. Whisk the egg whites and the rest of the salt together in a separate bowl until they form soft peaks – make sure they don't get too stiff or they won't blend in with the rest of the mixture. Fold 1 large tablespoon of whites into the zucchini mixture to loosen it slightly and then gently fold in the remainder. Pour about ½ inch (1 cm) of sunflower oil into a large skillet. Using half the mixture, drop in 2 large spoonfuls of the batter, spacing them a little apart, and fry for 3–4 minutes on each side over a medium heat until golden. Drain on paper towels and keep warm in the oven while you cook the other 2 and then cook the salmon.

Heat a skillet until it is very hot. Add a splash of oil and the salmon and sear for 3 minutes on each side. Lift onto a baking sheet and season with a little lemon juice, salt, and pepper.

To finish the dish, put the olive oil for the vinaigrette into a small pan with the diced red pepper and leave over a very low heat for a couple of minutes to let the flavor infuse the oil. Add the lobster and the tomatoes and warm through. Stir in the cilantro, basil, balsamic vinegar, and some seasoning. Place a zucchini fritter in the center of each warmed plate and rest a piece of the salmon on top. Spoon a little of the lobster vinaigrette around the edge of the plate and serve.

GRIDDLED TROUT

with herb *beurre blanc*

The real secret of this lies in spanking-fresh, native brown trout. In the TV series I managed to cook one that had been caught only 20 minutes earlier, and it was – well, you can guess! For maximum flavor, trout should be less than 24 hours out of the water, making them firm, glossy, and flavorsome. This is the perfect dish for a river or loch-side barbecue. The butter sauce is easy, once you've got the knack, and goes with all kinds of fish. Then you can experiment with different herbs, spices, pastes, and purées for flavoring it.

Serves 4

Maldon or sea salt and freshly ground
    white pepper
4 brown trout (or rainbow trout), cleaned
    and trimmed
olive oil
juice of ½ lemon

For the herb *beurre blanc*:
2 shallots, very finely chopped
3 tablespoons dry white wine
3 tablespoons white wine vinegar
6 white peppercorns, lightly crushed
¾ cup chilled unsalted butter, diced
2 tablespoons chopped fresh tarragon

For the *beurre blanc*, put the shallots, white wine, vinegar, and peppercorns into a small pan and boil rapidly until reduced to about 2 tablespoons of liquid. Reduce the heat to low and whisk in the butter, a few pieces at a time, to give a smooth, velvety sauce. Season with salt and pepper. Pass through a fine sieve into another pan and keep warm in a bowl of warm water while you cook the fish.

Heat a ridged, cast-iron griddle until very hot. Season the trout inside and out. Drizzle a little olive oil over the griddle, add the fish, and cook for 4 minutes on each side.

Season the fish once more and squeeze over a little lemon juice. Transfer to warmed plates. Add the chopped tarragon to the sauce and spoon some over the trout, putting the rest to one side of the fish.

SEARED FILLET OF TURBOT

on a bed of braised peas, lettuce, and bacon

I'm particularly fond of this combination of salty bacon, sweet peas, and lettuce, and fried fish. You can use romaine lettuce or crisp head lettuce hearts, or even iceberg at a push. If fresh peas aren't available, then frozen petits pois make a good substitute, but reduce the chicken stock for 3 minutes before adding them and then cook them for just 3 minutes before adding the lettuce. The garnish also works well with other firm-fleshed fish, such as halibut, monkfish, John Dory, or brill.

Serves 4

1 tablespoon sunflower oil

1 tablespoon Clarified Butter (see page 183)

4 (6 oz) (175 g) fillets of turbot

lemon juice

Maldon or sea salt and freshly ground
    white pepper

For the braised peas, lettuce, and bacon:

1 tablespoon extra-virgin olive oil

½ cup chopped rindless bacon or pancetta

2 tablespoons butter

½ onion, very finely chopped

1 small clove garlic, crushed

2½ cups shelled fresh peas or frozen
    petits pois

a pinch of superfine sugar

6 tablespoons Chicken Stock (see page 181)
    or water

2 romaine or crisp head lettuce hearts, finely
    shredded

2 tablespoons chopped fresh chives

For the braised peas, heat the olive oil in a pan, add the bacon, and fry until crisp and lightly golden. Add the butter and onion and cook for another 2–3 minutes until the onion has softened and is very lightly browned. Add the garlic, peas, sugar, stock or water, and some seasoning; cover and cook over a gentle heat for 6 minutes if using fresh peas and about 3 minutes if using frozen, until they are tender.

Heat the sunflower oil in a large skillet. Add the clarified butter and the turbot fillets and fry over a high heat for 3–4 minutes on each side until just cooked through. Lift them out of the pan onto a plate to prevent them from cooking any further. Season with a little lemon juice, salt and pepper, and keep warm.

Stir the shredded lettuce and chives into the peas and cook for 1 more minute. Check the peas for seasoning and then spoon the mixture into the centers of 4 warmed plates. Place the turbot fillets on top and serve.

STEAMED FLOUNDER

with green onions, ginger, and chili

Now here's something else that I'd never cooked before, so I looked it up in my fish books, which were all unanimous in pronouncing the poor old flounder a second-rate fish. Well, I have to take them to task because with the addition of all these zingy Chinese flavors it is really rather good. To serve four, simply double up the pans and ingredients.

Serves 2

1 inch (2.5 cm) piece ginger root, peeled

3 green onions, trimmed

½–1 long, thin red chili pepper

1 clove garlic

1 lime

2 tablespoons good-quality light soy sauce

2 teaspoons sesame oil

2 tablespoons olive oil, plus extra for the
    noodles

¼ cup chopped fresh chives, plus extra to
    garnish

freshly ground white pepper

1 (1½ lb) (675 g) flounder, filleted or left whole

4 oz (100 g) medium, dried egg noodles

Bring 2 pots of water to a boil. Make sure one of them is the right size to support either a plate or a bamboo steamer.

Cut the piece of ginger into fine julienne strips. Thinly slice the green onions on the diagonal, thinly slice the chili pepper, chop the garlic, and squeeze the juice from half of the lime. Cut the other piece of lime in half once more and set aside.

The easiest way to prepare the fish for steaming is to place a large sheet of plastic wrap over the plate or into the bottom of the steamer, so that the edges are left overhanging. Place half of the following flavorings and oils: ginger, green onions, chili pepper, garlic, lime juice, soy sauce, sesame and olive oils in the center of the plastic wrap and add a large pinch of chopped chives and some white pepper. Lay the fish (or fish fillets) on top. Sprinkle over the remainder of the flavorings and the oils and then gather in the edges of the plastic wrap and twist them together over the top of the fish to make a watertight package where none of the juices can leak out. Rest the fish on top of one of the pans of water, cover and cook for 8–10 minutes.

After the fish has been cooking for 4 minutes, drop the noodles into the second pan of water and add a few drops of olive oil. Bring back to a boil, cover and set aside off the heat for 4 minutes. Drain the noodles well and return them to the pan.

Lift the fish off the steamer with a fish slice or slotted spoon, hold it over the pan of noodles, and carefully undo the plastic wrap. Let all the cooking juices drip into the noodles. Set down the fish and toss the noodles with the juices. Swirl them into the center of a large serving plate (for a whole fish) or 2 serving plates (for fillets) and place the fish on top. Season lightly, sprinkle with the rest of the chopped chives, and serve with the remaining pieces of lime for squeezing.

STEAMED COD ON A BED OF WILTED SPINACH

with a tomato and blood orange dressing

This dish was developed as part of a healthy eating demonstration which I gave in Glasgow. The fact that the attendance topped the 850 mark reinforced in my mind just how conscious people are these days of eating healthily. Well, you can rest easy with this dish – provided it's served with some plain boiled new potatoes (add a couple of tablespoons of chopped basil for extra flavor), it meets all Glasgow University's criteria for a perfectly balanced meal. And oh, it tastes not bad either. For cooking the cod, you can use a purpose-made steamer consisting of two pans stacked one on top of the other, a bamboo steamer resting over a large saucepan or skillet, or a plate resting on an upturned bowl placed in the bottom of a larger saucepan. Whichever you choose must be covered with a well-fitting lid so that the fish cooks in hot steam.

Serves 4

4 (6 oz) (175 g) pieces thick cod fillet, unskinned

2 tablespoons olive oil

2–3 cloves garlic, crushed

1 lb (450 g) fresh spinach, washed and any large stalks removed

2 tablespoons freshly squeezed lemon juice

Maldon or sea salt and freshly ground black pepper

For the tomato and blood orange dressing:

8 oz (225 g) cherry tomatoes

2 tablespoons blood orange juice

1 tablespoon extra-virgin olive oil

For the dressing, put the cherry tomatoes, blood orange juice, and olive oil into a blender and blitz everything for a few seconds until the tomatoes have just broken up. Press back into a small pan through a chinois or very fine sieve to get rid of all the skin and the little seeds, and season to taste. Set to one side while you cook the fish and the spinach.

Pour some water into your steamer and bring it to a boil. Add the fish, skin-side up, cover with a tight-fitting lid, and steam for 7–8 minutes until just firm and opaque. Meanwhile, heat the oil in a large pan. Add the garlic and fry for about 1 minute. Add the prepared spinach and stir-fry over a high heat until it has wilted down into the bottom of the pan. Tip it into a colander and press out the excess water. Return it to the pan with half the lemon juice and some seasoning, and stir over a medium heat until it has just heated through. At the same time, place the pan of blood orange dressing over a low heat and let it warm through to blood temperature, but do not let it boil.

To serve, spoon the spinach into the centers of 4 warmed plates. Lift the cod out of the steamer and peel the skin off each piece. Season with the remaining lemon juice and salt and pepper, and place on top of the spinach. Pour some of the dressing over and around the fish.

POTATO AND MACKEREL CURRY

with cardamom rice

This may seem a bit complicated for a curry, where you would normally fling everything into the pot and let it bubble away. However, by cooking the fish, potatoes, and sauce separately and then bringing them together at the end, you avoid having a pot of fish and potato glue at the end. If you want to make this in advance, keep all the ingredients separate until ready to serve, then reheat together while the rice is cooking.

Serves 4

1 lb (450 g) waxy main-crop potatoes

2 whole cloves

1 teaspoon each of fennel, cumin, and
   coriander seeds

a very small piece cinnamon stick

½ teaspoon ground turmeric

2 (12 oz–1 lb) (350–450 g) mackerel, filleted

2 tablespoons all-purpose flour, seasoned with
   ¼ teaspoon Maldon or sea salt and freshly
   ground black pepper

5 tablespoons peanut or sunflower oil

12 oz (350 g) onions (about 2 medium),
   chopped

1 inch (2.5 cm) piece fresh ginger root,
   peeled and finely grated

2–3 green chilies, seeded and finely chopped

¾ teaspoon Maldon or sea salt

¾ cup Greek natural yogurt

1¼ cups Fish Stock (see page 180)

3 tablespoons chopped fresh cilantro

For the cardamom rice:

1⅓ cups basmati rice

1 tablespoon butter

6 green cardamom pods, cracked

½ teaspoon Maldon or sea salt

1½ cups boiling water

Boil the unpeeled potatoes until they are tender when pierced with a skewer (about 25 minutes). Meanwhile, heat a dry, heavy-bottomed skillet until it is very hot. Add the cloves, fennel, cumin and coriander seeds, and cinnamon stick, and dry-roast for a minute or two until they darken slightly and start to smell aromatic. Tip them into a coffee grinder or mortar and grind to a fine powder. Stir in the ground turmeric powder. Drain the potatoes and leave to cool, then peel them and cut into ¾ inch (2 cm) chunks. Set aside.

Coat the mackerel fillets in the seasoned flour. Heat about 3–4 tablespoons of the oil in a large, deep skillet or shallow casserole. Add the fillets and fry for a couple of minutes on each side until golden brown. Carefully lift out onto a plate and set aside.

Add the potatoes to the pan and cook over a medium heat until they are nicely golden on all sides. Lift out and set aside. Add the rest of the oil to the pan, add the onions, ginger, and green chilies, and fry for 5–6 minutes until the onions are soft and lightly browned.

Meanwhile, put the rice into a sieve and rinse under cold water until the water runs clear. Tip into a bowl, cover with cold water, and leave to soak for 5 minutes. Heat the butter in a pan, add the cardamom pods, and fry for 1 minute. Drain the rice, add to the pan, and stir gently until all the grains are coated in the butter. Add the salt and boiling water. Bring to a boil, cover and cook over a low heat for 12 minutes. Remove from the heat and leave to stand until the curry is ready.

Break the mackerel fillets into chunky pieces. Add the prepared spices and ¾ teaspoon salt to the onions and cook for 1 minute. Now add the yogurt, 1 large spoonful at a time, frying it for a minute or two between each addition. Stir in the fish stock and then return the potatoes and the mackerel pieces to the pan, together with half the chopped cilantro. Simmer for 3–4 minutes until the fish is just cooked through. Sprinkle with the rest of the chopped cilantro and serve with the cardamom rice.

SEARED CRAWFISH

with tomato, basil, and lemon couscous

Crawfish, sometimes called spiny lobster are the big bruisers of the shellfish world. Unfortunately they are not that widely available, though you might hit it lucky with a good fish merchant – but then comes the heart-stopping price. So unless you're a lottery winner, substitute lobster or raw tiger shrimp.

Serves 4

2 (2 lb) (900 g) crawfish

Generous 1 cup Marinated Vegetable Stock (see page 179), Fish Stock (see page 180), or water

1 cup couscous

6 Home-dried Tomatoes (see page 184), diced

3 tablespoons olive oil, plus extra for searing the crawfish and dressing the salad

juice of ½ lemon, plus 1 teaspoon

2 tablespoons chopped fresh basil

Maldon or sea salt and freshly ground white pepper

About ½ cup mixed salad leaves, such as frisée lettuce, dandelion, arugula, and chives

¼ cup Herb Oil (see page 186)

Drop the crawfish into a large pan of boiling water and cook for 8 minutes. Lift out, drop into a pan or sink full of cold water, and leave to cool. Crack open the tail shells and carefully take out the meat.

Bring the stock or water to a boil in a pan. Slowly pour in the couscous, give it a good stir, and then add the tomatoes, the 3 tablespoons of olive oil, the juice of ½ a lemon, and the basil. Cover, take off the heat, and leave to stand for 5 minutes. Fluff up the grains with a fork and season to taste with some salt and pepper.

Cut the crawfish tail meat into about 16 medallions. Heat a little more olive oil in a large frying pan. When it is very hot, add the medallions a few at a time and sear for 1 minute on each side. Keep warm while you sear the rest.

Divide the couscous between 4 warmed serving plates (you can spoon it into a 3 inch (7.5 cm) pastry cutter to give it nice tower-shapes if you wish) and place the medallions around it.

Place the salad leaves in a bowl and dress with the rest of the lemon juice, a few drops of olive oil, and some seasoning. Pile the leaves on top of the couscous, drizzle the herb oil around the edge of the plate, and serve.

CRAB CAKES

with lobster mayonnaise and salad

I've made the mayonnaise with lobster oil for its intense flavor but, if you haven't got any or can't be bothered with the hassle of making it, this dish is still very tasty made with good-quality store-bought mayonnaise. Just add a crushed clove of garlic to the mix to help things along. You could use frozen or pasteurized crabmeat for the cakes but it's worth the effort to get fresh. The simplest and easiest way to do this is to buy crab claws only (without the body which is fiddly to shell) and ask the fish merchant to crack them for you.

Serves 4

juice of ½ lemon (about 1 ½ tablespoons)
1 lb (450 g) fresh white crabmeat
1 long, thin red chili pepper, finely chopped (seeds and all)
3 tablespoons chopped fresh cilantro
Maldon or sea salt and freshly ground white pepper
4 cups fresh white breadcrumbs

sunflower oil for shallow-frying
3 oz (75 g) baby salad leaves
a little olive oil

For the lobster mayonnaise:

1 medium farm-fresh egg yolk
1 tablespoon Dijon mustard
1 ¼ cups Lobster Oil (see page 187)
2 tablespoons warm water

First make the lobster mayonnaise. Mix the egg yolk and mustard together in a small bowl. Very gradually whisk in the lobster oil so that the mixture becomes thick and glossy. Spoon 4 tablespoons into another small bowl and stir in the warm water to thin it down into a sauce. Cover and set aside in the refrigerator.

For the crab cakes, put another 4 tablespoons of the mayonnaise into a bowl and whisk in the lemon juice. The rest of the mayonnaise can be stored in the refrigerator for 3–4 days. Fold in the crabmeat, chili pepper, and cilantro, and season to taste with salt and pepper. Form the mixture into eight 2 inch (5 cm) flat discs and then roll them in the breadcrumbs so that they take on a good, thick, even coating. Place them on a baking sheet, cover and chill for 1–2 hours to set.

When you are ready to cook the crab cakes, heat about ¼ inch (5 mm) sunflower oil in a large, heavy-bottomed skillet. Add the crab cakes and fry them for 3–4 minutes on each side until golden. Toss the salad leaves with a few drops of olive oil and some seasoning. Pile the salad leaves into the centers of 4 plates and place the crab cakes on top. Drizzle around the lobster mayonnaise and serve.

BAKED POTATOES

with spinach, Arbroath smokies, and poached eggs

These are just posh baked tatties. If possible, use nice, big, floury main-crop potatoes such as Idaho. The best bit about this dish is when you cut into the poached egg and the yolk runs down into the smoky, fishy potato filling. Tasty, very, very tasty – but slimming food this is not!

Serves 4

4 large floury baking potatoes such as Idaho
1 lb (450 g) Arbroath smokies, or lightly smoked small haddock
5 tablespoons butter
10 oz (275 g) baby leaf spinach

Maldon or sea salt and freshly ground black pepper
1 tablespoon chopped fresh chives
1 tablespoon chopped fresh flat-leaf parsley
¼ cup finely grated Parmesan
4 medium farm-fresh eggs
a few long-cut fresh chives, to garnish

Bake the potatoes at 375°F (190°C) for 1½ hours. Meanwhile, skin and bone the haddock and break the flesh into small pieces.

When the potatoes are nearly ready, heat 1 tablespoon of the butter in a large pan. Add the spinach and stir-fry over a high heat for a few minutes until it has wilted into the bottom of the pan. Tip it into a colander and press out the excess water. Transfer to a cutting board, sprinkle with some salt and pepper, and roughly chop.

Remove the potatoes from the oven and cut each one in half. Scoop out most of the flesh into a bowl, leaving behind enough to hold the skins in shape. Mash the potato with the rest of the butter and then stir in the flaked fish, chopped herbs, and some seasoning. Divide the spinach between each potato shell and spread out with the back of a spoon. Cover with the potato mixture and flatten the tops; sprinkle over the grated cheese and place on the rack of the broiler pan.

Preheat the broiler to high. Meanwhile, pour about 1½ inches (4 cm) water into a large skillet and place it over a gentle heat. Slide the baked potatoes under the broiler and cook for a few minutes until the cheese is golden and bubbling. As soon as little bubbles escape from the water in the skillet, carefully break in the eggs and poach for 3 minutes, basting the top of the eggs with a little of the hot water as they cook. Lift them out with a slotted spoon and drain briefly on some paper towels. Place 2 baked potato halves on each plate, top with the poached eggs, and garnish with a few chives.

POULTRY AND GAME

SWEET CHILI CHICKEN KEBABS

Eating with your fingertips is a most underrated sensuous experience and barbecued kebabs are a most underrated dish. Here are four chances to redress the balance. You can thread the kebabs in advance for all these recipes.

These kebabs are quite spicy and, if you can stand the heat, they are great assembled with some extra pieces of seeded red chili threaded onto the skewers along with the chicken. You can also serve them very simply with a fresh tomato and oregano salad and some thin, crisp French fries.

Serves 4

3 large chicken breasts, skinned and boned
2 small red onions
8 small, fresh bay leaves

For the sweet chili marinade:
1 long, thin red chili pepper, seeded and very
    finely chopped

3 tablespoons olive oil
1½ tablespoons sweet red chili sauce
2 teaspoons lemon juice
1 tablespoon chopped fresh oregano
1 clove garlic, crushed
Maldon or sea salt and freshly ground
    black pepper

Remove any little fillets from the underside of each piece of chicken; then cut each breast lengthwise into 4 long strips. Peel the onions, leaving the root ends intact. Cut each one into 6 thin wedges through the root so that the wedges stay together in one piece.

Mix together the ingredients for the marinade. Put the chicken, red onion wedges, and bay leaves into a bowl; stir in the marinade and leave at room temperature for 2 hours or overnight in the refrigerator.

If you are going to barbecue your kebabs, allow about 40 minutes for the coals to reach the right temperature. If you are broiling your kebabs, preheat your broiler to medium–high. Soak bamboo skewers, if using, for 30 minutes. Thread 3 strips of chicken alternately with 3 red onion wedges and 2 bay leaves onto four 10 inch (25 cm) metal or bamboo skewers. Cook on a barbecue or under a broiler for 6–8 minutes, turning now and then, until cooked through but still juicy.

MARJORAM AND LEMON CHICKEN KEBABS

with a tomato, basil, and lemon pilaf

I've used chicken thighs in this recipe as I find the acidity of the lemon dries out breast meat too much. They're also tastier than breast meat and the extra fat bastes them during barbecuing, which is my favorite way of cooking them.

Serves 4

6 chicken thighs, skinned and boned

20 small cherry tomatoes

2 tablespoons chopped fresh marjoram

2 cloves garlic, crushed

finely grated zest and juice of 1 large lemon

3 tablespoons olive oil

Maldon or sea salt and freshly ground
   black pepper

For the tomato, basil and lemon pilaf:

1 small onion, finely chopped

1–2 tablespoons olive oil

1 clove garlic, crushed

½ cup sun-dried tomatoes in oil, drained and
   roughly chopped

1¾ cups long-grain rice

1¼ cups tomato purée

1¼ cups Chicken Stock
   (see page 181)

finely grated zest of ½ small lemon

1 tablespoon lemon juice

3 tablespoons finely shredded fresh basil

Cut each chicken thigh into 4 pieces. Place in a bowl with all the other kebab ingredients, cover and leave to marinate at room temperature for 2 hours or in the refrigerator overnight.

Soak bamboo skewers, if using, for 30 minutes. If you are going to barbecue your kebabs, allow about 40 minutes for the coals to reach the right temperature. If you are broiling your kebabs, preheat your broiler to medium–high after you have threaded the skewers.

For the pilaf, sauté the onion in the oil for 5 minutes until lightly browned. Add the garlic and fry for another minute. Stir in the sun-dried tomatoes and the rice thoroughly so that all the grains of rice get nicely coated in the oil. Stir in the tomato purée and the stock. Bring up to a boil, cover and cook over a low heat for 20 minutes. Meanwhile, thread 6 pieces of chicken and 5 cherry tomatoes alternately onto four 10 inch (25 cm) metal or bamboo skewers.

When the pilaf is halfway through cooking, cook the kebabs on the barbecue or under the broiler for 6–8 minutes, turning now and then, until golden brown. Uncover the pilaf and fork in the lemon zest, lemon juice, basil, and some salt and pepper to taste. Spoon the pilaf into the center of 4 warmed plates and arrange the kebabs on top.

CHICKEN SATAY KEBABS
with spicy peanut sauce and Thai noodles

Another variation on the kebab theme, satay is great because the skewers can be threaded up in advance and kept on a tray, covered in plastic wrap, until ready for cooking. Satay is now a widely appreciated flavor in Britain, but the first time I tasted it was in the late 1970s in Singapore and I remember thinking it was the most exotic and delicious thing ever. I've tried many times to recapture that original flavor, but never quite got there. This comes pretty close, though.

Serves 4

6 large chicken breasts, skinned and boned

For the marinade:
1½ teaspoons cumin seeds
1½ teaspoons coriander seeds
½ teaspoon dried chili flakes
1 large clove garlic, crushed
1 tablespoon light soy sauce
2 teaspoons light brown sugar
a good pinch of turmeric powder
¼ cup canned coconut milk
1 tablespoon lime juice

For the spicy peanut sauce:
¼ cup natural roasted peanuts (that is, no added fat or salt)
3 cloves garlic, crushed
3 shallots, peeled and chopped

1 long, thin red chili pepper, seeded and chopped
2 teaspoons paprika
1½ tablespoons sunflower oil
¾ cup canned coconut milk
1 tablespoon light brown sugar
½ teaspoon Maldon or sea salt or to taste

For the Thai noodles:
3 oz (75 g) rice vermicelli (also known as stir-fry noodles)
juice of 1 lime
1 long, thin red chili pepper, seeded and finely chopped
6 green onions, trimmed and thinly sliced
1 clove garlic, finely chopped
2 teaspoons sesame oil
2 teaspoons sunflower oil
1½ tablespoons Thai fish sauce
2 tablespoons chopped fresh cilantro

Cut the chicken into 1½ inch (4 cm) chunks. For the marinade, heat a dry, heavy-bottomed skillet until hot, add the cumin and coriander seeds and chili flakes, and toss around for a few seconds until they darken slightly and start to smell aromatic. Grind to a fine powder in a coffee grinder or with a mortar and pestle. Set aside 1 teaspoon for the sauce. Mix the rest with the remaining marinade ingredients in a bowl, stir in the chicken pieces, and leave to marinate at room temperature for 2 hours or up to 24 hours in the refrigerator.

Shortly before you are about to cook the kebabs, soak the bamboo skewers, if using, for 10 minutes and make the spicy peanut sauce. Grind the peanuts to a fine powder and set them aside. Put the reserved cumin, coriander, and chili powder into a coffee grinder with the garlic, shallots, chopped chili pepper, and paprika, and whizz to a smooth paste. Heat the oil in a small pan, add the paste, and cook over a medium heat for 3 minutes. Add the coconut milk, ground peanuts, sugar, and salt. Bring up to a gentle simmer and simmer for 2 minutes. Leave to cool slightly.

If you are going to barbecue your kebabs, allow about 40 minutes for the coals to reach the right temperature. If you are broiling your kebabs, preheat your broiler to medium–high. Bring a large pan of lightly salted water to a boil. Thread the chicken pieces onto metal or pre-soaked bamboo skewers and cook for 8 minutes, turning them now and then, until lightly browned but still moist and juicy in the center. Meanwhile, drop the noodles into the boiling water, take the pan off the heat, and leave them to soak for 3 minutes. Drain them well and leave to cool slightly; then toss with the rest of the noodle ingredients.

Spoon the warm peanut sauce into 4 small dipping saucers or ramekins and serve with the kebabs and the noodles.

MOROCCAN CHICKEN KEBABS

with dates and bacon on a bed of spiced couscous

This final kebab variation looks to North Africa and the delightful sweet and spicy flavors found there. Do try and get fresh medjool dates, they taste so good.

Serves 4

4 chicken breasts, skinned and boned

2 tablespoons olive oil

1 tablespoon lemon juice

1 teaspoon ground cumin

1 teaspoon ground coriander

½ teaspoon turmeric powder

½ teaspoon paprika

½ teaspoon ground cinnamon

1 teaspoon soft light brown sugar

1 teaspoon harissa paste or minced red chili
   pepper paste from a jar

2 cloves garlic, crushed

12 fresh medjool dates

6 slices rindless streaky bacon, cut in half

12 no-need-to-soak dried apricots

Maldon or sea salt and freshly ground
   black pepper

For the spiced couscous:

3 tablespoons olive oil

1 medium onion, finely chopped

1 large clove garlic, finely chopped

1½ teaspoons ground cumin

1½ teaspoons ground coriander

1½ teaspoons ground paprika

½ teaspoon turmeric powder

1½ cups Chicken Stock
   (see page 181)

1⅓ cups couscous

6 green onions, trimmed and thinly sliced

2 long, thin red chili peppers, seeded and
   finely chopped

½ cup toasted pine nuts

finely grated zest and juice of 1 lemon

1½ tablespoons chopped fresh cilantro

1½ tablespoons chopped fresh mint

Cut the chicken into 1½ inch (4 cm) pieces. Place in a bowl with all the kebab ingredients except the dates, bacon, and apricots. Season with a little salt and pepper. Toss together well, cover and leave to marinate at room temperature for 2 hours or up to 24 hours in the refrigerator.

Soak bamboo skewers, if using, for 30 minutes. Make a slit in the side of each date and hook out the pits with the tip of a knife. Stretch each piece of bacon with the side of a kitchen knife and then wrap each one around a date. Thread the pieces of chicken, bacon-wrapped dates, and apricots alternately onto 4 metal or bamboo skewers and set to one side.

If you are going to barbecue your kebabs, allow about 40 minutes for the coals to reach the right temperature. If you are broiling your kebabs, preheat your broiler to medium–high. Cook the kebabs for 10–12 minutes, turning them every now and then, until the bacon is crisp and the chicken is cooked through but still moist and juicy in the center. Keep the kebabs warm.

Next, prepare the couscous. Heat half the oil in a medium-size pan. Add the onion and cook until it is soft and lightly browned. Add the garlic and cook for 1 minute; then stir in all the spices and fry for another minute. Add the stock and bring it to a boil. Pour in the couscous in a slow, steady stream, bring it up to a boil, and stir once more. Cover, take the pan off the heat and set it aside for 5 minutes. Now uncover the pan and fork up the couscous into separate fluffy grains. Fork in the rest of the oil and the remaining couscous ingredients and season to taste with salt and pepper.

Spoon the couscous slightly off-center onto 4 warmed plates and rest a kebab alongside each portion.

HARISSA CHICKEN

with couscous and lemon and cumin yogurt

Harissa is a fiery red chili paste from Morocco, but if you can't find it easily, you can successfully substitute a ground red chili paste which is available in many supermarkets now. This harissa coating will also work well on racks of lamb. Just roast them for 12–15 minutes. It will darken a little more than when you use it with chicken because there is no skin to protect it, but it will still taste just as good.

Serves 4

2 cloves garlic, crushed

1 tablespoon harissa paste or red chili pepper paste from a jar

2 tablespoons olive oil

⅓ cup sun-dried tomatoes in oil, very finely chopped

1 teaspoon chopped fresh thyme

Maldon or sea salt and ½ teaspoon coarsely ground black pepper

4 large chicken suprêmes (that is, with the little wing bone still attached)

a little extra-virgin olive oil, to serve

Maldon or sea salt and freshly ground black pepper

2 teaspoons cumin seeds

2 teaspoons coriander seeds

¼ teaspoon fennel seeds

¼ teaspoon turmeric powder

2 cloves garlic, finely chopped

1¼ cups Chicken Stock (see page 181)

1⅓ cups couscous

⅓ cup golden raisins

½ cup toasted pine nuts

3 tablespoons lemon juice

1 tablespoon chopped fresh oregano

1 tablespoon chopped fresh flat-leaf parsley

For the couscous:

2 medium onions, peeled and cut into wedges through the roots

2 red bell peppers, seeded and cut into quarters

4 tablespoons olive oil

a pinch of superfine sugar

For the lemon and cumin yogurt:

1 tablespoon sunflower oil

1 teaspoon cumin seeds

6 tablespoons natural Greek or whole-milk yogurt

finely grated zest of ½ small lemon

2 teaspoons lemon juice

a pinch of Maldon or sea salt

Preheat the oven to 425°F (220°C). For the couscous, mix the onion wedges, red peppers, 2 tablespoons of the olive oil, sugar, and some seasoning together in a small roasting pan. Then prepare the chicken flavorings. Mix together the crushed garlic, harissa paste or minced red chili paste , olive oil, sun-dried tomatoes, thyme, ½ teaspoon coarsely ground black pepper, and a little salt. Loosen the skin of each chicken suprême, leaving it attached along one long edge, and spread the harissa mixture under the skin of each one in an even layer. Replace the skin and secure the open edge with a fine trussing skewer or a wooden toothpick which has been soaked in cold water for 30 minutes. Place the chicken pieces in another small roasting pan.

Slide the pan of vegetables into the oven and roast for 10 minutes. Then slide the pan of chicken alongside and roast for another 20–25 minutes.

Meanwhile, heat a dry, heavy-bottomed skillet over a high heat. Add the cumin, coriander, and fennel seeds, and dry-roast them until they darken slightly and start to smell aromatic. Grind them to a fine powder in a coffee grinder or with a mortar and pestle; then stir in the tumeric powder.

For the lemon and cumin yogurt, heat the oil in a small pan. Add the cumin seeds and as soon as they start to pop, tip them into the yogurt. Add the lemon zest, lemon juice, and salt and mix together well. Cover and leave in the refrigerator to chill.

Remove the chicken and vegetables from the oven. Leave the chicken somewhere warm to relax. Remove the skin from the pieces of red pepper and then cut them into small pieces together with the onions. Heat another tablespoon of oil in a pan, add the chopped garlic and the ground, dry-roasted spices, and fry for 30 seconds. Add the stock and bring to a boil. Stir in the couscous and the golden raisins. Bring back to a boil and remove from the heat. Cover and leave to steam for 5 minutes. Now fluff up the grains with a fork and fork in the rest of the oil, the roasted vegetables, pine kernels, lemon juice, chopped oregano and parsley, and seasoning to taste.

Carve the chicken into diagonal slices. Spoon the couscous into the centers of 4 warmed plates and place the chicken on top. Spoon some of the cumin and yogurt dressing around the edge of each plate and then drizzle around a little extra-virgin olive oil.

ROAST PARTRIDGE

with garlic baby kale, deep-fried parsnip shreds, and game gravy

I always tended to think of kale as animal feed, but the baby leaves stir-fried with garlic are just sublime – full of flavor and with a lovely crunchy texture. Partridge is one of my favorite game birds, in season in Britain from September 1 to February1; it has a paler flesh than most other game birds. If you haven't been shooting this weekend, guinea fowl makes a good substitute.

Serves 4

6 small, plump partridges
Maldon or sea salt and freshly ground
   black pepper
1–2 tablespoons sunflower oil

For the game gravy:
1 tablespoon sunflower oil
4 small shallots, peeled and chopped
1 carrot, peeled and chopped
2 oz (50 g) mushrooms, sliced
1 clove garlic, crushed
1 fresh bay leaf
1 sprig of fresh thyme

6 white peppercorns, crushed
1¼ cups red or white wine
1 teaspoon red currant jelly
2½ cups Chicken Stock (see page 181)
1¼ cups Beef Stock (see page 182)

For the deep-fried parsnip shreds:
sunflower oil for deep frying
2–3 small parsnips, peeled

For the garlic baby kale:
1 tablespoon sunflower oil
2 cloves garlic, cut into very fine shreds
1 lb (450 g) baby kale, washed and dried

First make the gravy. Remove the breasts from the partridges and remove the skin from each one. Cut the rest of the carcasses into small pieces. Heat the oil in a large pan and add the carcasses, shallots, carrot, mushrooms, garlic, bay leaf, thyme, and peppercorns. Fry over a high heat, stirring now and then, until everything is richly golden. Add the wine and boil until it has reduced to a couple of tablespoons. Add the red currant jelly and the chicken and beef stock, and simmer until reduced to about 1¼ cups. Strain through a sieve into a clean pan, pressing out as much liquid as you can with the back of a ladle. Taste the gravy and season with salt and a little more pepper if necessary. Set aside.

Preheat the oven to 450°F (230°C). For the parsnip shreds, pour some oil into a medium-sized pan until it is about one-third full. Heat to 350°F (180°C). Meanwhile, peel each parsnip lengthwise with a sharp potato peeler into long paper-thin strips, turning it every now and then, until you reach the hard central core, which you have to discard. As soon as the oil is ready, drop in a handful of the parsnip shreds and fry for 1 minute until crisp and golden. Lift out with a slotted spoon and drain on paper towels. Repeat with the rest of the parsnip shreds.

Now it's time to cook the partridge breasts. Season them well on both sides with salt and pepper. Heat a flameproof, heavy-bottomed skillet until it is very hot. Add the oil and the partridge breasts and fry for 2 minutes on either side until richly golden. Turn the breasts rounded-side up, slide the pan into the oven and roast for 3 minutes until they are cooked but still slightly pink in the center. Remove from the oven and leave somewhere warm to relax. Place the gravy over a low heat and leave to warm through.

For the kale, heat the oil in a wok or large pan and add the garlic. Fry for a few seconds until it starts to color. Add the kale and stir-fry over a high heat for about 1 minute. Remove the pan from the heat and season with salt and pepper. Spoon 3 small piles of the kale into the centers of 4 warmed plates. Place a partridge breast on top of each pile of kale. Spoon some of the gravy around the edge of each plate and then pile plenty of parsnip shreds in the center.

PAN-FRIED PIGEON BREASTS

with baby bok choy and chili and black bean sauce

This, for me, is a real fusion dish. Normally I would serve game with autumnal garnishes, such as cabbage, lentils, root vegetables, or barley but, here the rich, meaty flavor goes really well with the Asian greens and the spicy chili juices. And there's no complicated sauce to make either. This will definitely be on the menu at my new restaurant, Nairns, in Glasgow!

Serves 4

8 wood pigeon breasts, skinned
Maldon or sea salt and freshly ground
    Szechwan peppercorns
5 tablespoons sunflower oil
12 oz (350g) baby bok choy
1 tablespoon light sesame oil

1 clove garlic, finely chopped
1 inch (2.5 cm) piece ginger root, peeled and
    finely chopped
2 tablespoons Chinese chili and black
    bean sauce
1 tablespoon lime juice
4 tablespoons Chicken Stock (see page 181)
2 tablespoons chopped fresh cilantro

Heat a large, heavy-bottomed skillet until it is very hot. Season the pigeon breasts with salt and Szechwan pepper. Add to the pan with 1 tablespoon of the oil and fry for about 2 minutes on each side. Lift onto a plate, cover and leave somewhere warm to relax .

Trim the bok choy and cut each one in half through the stem. Add the sesame oil and the rest of the sunflower oil, garlic, and ginger to the pan and fry for 1–2 minutes. Add the bok choy and stir-fry for 1 minute. Add the chili and black bean sauce, lime juice, stock, and chopped cilantro and shake around for about 30 seconds.

Lift the bok choy out of the juices and pile into the centers of 4 warmed plates. Slice each pigeon breast thinly and lay on top of the bok choy. Taste the cooking juices left in the pan and season to taste. Spoon them around the edge of the plate and serve.

ROAST MEDALLIONS OF VENISON

with a confit of carrots and celery

To make a proper confit, you slow-braise meat or vegetables in duck fat. What I've done here is to slow-roast pieces of root vegetables in a little seasoned olive oil. To ensure even browning, you need to stir and turn the vegetables several times during cooking. This process produces a richer and more intense flavor than conventional cooking methods, and the taste works particularly well with the rich flavor of game, making a perfect winter warmer.

Serves 6

6 (5 oz) (150 g) medallions of venison (bones and trimmings reserved for the jus)
Maldon or sea salt and freshly ground white pepper
2 tablespoons olive oil

For the red wine jus:

5 tablespoons olive oil
4 stalks celery, roughly chopped
1 large onion, unpeeled and quartered
2 carrots, roughly chopped
1 head garlic, halved
4 shallots, roughly chopped
2 oz (50 g) mushrooms, roughly chopped
a sprig of fresh thyme

2 tablespoons butter
1 (7 oz) (200 g) can chopped tomatoes
½ bottle red wine
2 tablespoons rowan jelly

For the stovie potatoes:

6 (4 oz) (100 g) potatoes
5 tablespoons butter

For the confit of carrots and celery:

6 carrots, peeled
4–6 stalks celery
2 tablespoons olive oil
1 clove garlic, finely chopped
1 tablespoon fresh thyme leaves

First make the red wine jus. Preheat the oven to 425°F (220°C). Heat a large roasting pan on the stove top. Add 3 tablespoons of the oil, the chopped up bones reserved from preparing the medallions, the celery, onion, and carrots. Stir around over a high heat until they have turned a rich golden brown. Slide the pan into the oven and leave everything to roast for 30 minutes.

Put the venison trimmings, garlic, shallots, mushrooms, thyme, the rest of the oil, and the butter into a large stock pot. Cook over a medium–high heat for about 15 minutes until everything has caramelized nicely. Add the chopped tomatoes and the roasted bones and vegetables from the pan. Return the pan to the stove top. Add the wine and deglaze by scraping up all the sticky

juices from the bottom. Pour the wine into the stock pot and boil rapidly until almost all of it has disappeared. Pour in enough water to cover the bones and leave everything to simmer gently for 3 hours, lifting off any white frothy fat every now and then as it rises to the surface. Strain the stock through a colander first and skim off any fat; then pass it once more through a chinois or fine sieve into a clean pan. Add the rowan jelly and boil rapidly until the liquid has reduced to a well-flavored, slightly syrupy jus. Set aside.

Lower the oven temperature to 350°F (180°C). For the stovie potatoes, slice off either end of each one so that they are all the same size and look like little barrels when sitting upright. Spread the butter over the bottom of a small roasting pan or heavy-bottomed, ovenproof skillet. Press in the potatoes, cut-side down and season well with salt and pepper. Cook on the stove top over a medium heat for about 15 minutes until golden brown. Turn them over, slide the pan into the oven and cook the potatoes for 1 hour.

For the confit of carrots and celery, cut the vegetables diagonally into large 2 inch (5 cm) chunks. Heat a heavy-bottomed skillet over a high heat. Add 1 tablespoon of oil and the carrots and fry until they are golden brown. Transfer them to a roasting pan and repeat with the celery. Add the celery, garlic, thyme leaves, and some seasoning to the carrots and set aside.

After the potatoes have been cooking for 40 minutes, season the medallions of venison on both sides with salt and pepper. Heat a heavy-bottomed skillet until very hot. Add the oil and the medallions and fry the venison for 3–4 minutes on each side until nicely browned. Cover the pan with aluminum foil and set it aside somewhere warm for 15 minutes to let the meat relax. Five minutes later slide the carrots and celery into the oven and roast for 10 minutes. Season the red wine jus to taste and leave over a low heat to warm through.

To serve, place one potato and a large spoonful of the carrot and celery confit on each plate. Rest a medallion of venison on top of the confit and sprinkle with a little salt. Spoon the red wine jus around the edge of each plate.

ROAST LOIN OF HARE

on truffled spinach with horseradish mash and truffle oil

The flavor of truffle is one that I love but, unless you've just won the lottery, it's not one that many of us can afford. However, truffle oil, which is now stocked in some larger supermarkets, will give you the flavor without the cost. It's not as refined as the real thing but still lends a nice flavor. For the mashed potatoes, try to use fresh horseradish if you can get it, but jarred horseradish sauce (not the creamed one) will do. And, finally, you can serve venison instead of hare with these flavors equally well.

Serves 4

1½ lb (675 g) floury potatoes, such as Idaho

3 tablespoons unsalted butter

2 tablespoons horseradish sauce

Maldon or sea salt and freshly ground
    white pepper

2½ tablespoons sunflower oil

4 hare loins, off the bone

2 lb (900 g) fresh spinach, washed and large
    stalks removed

2 teaspoons truffle oil, plus extra to serve

1 tablespoon olive oil

a little fresh black or white truffle, very finely
    diced (optional)

Peel the potatoes and cut them into chunks. Cook them in boiling salted water for 20 minutes or until tender.

Drain the potatoes and leave them in the colander until all the steam has disappeared. Drop them back into the pan and cook over a low heat for a few minutes to get rid of any more moisture. Mash them by hand, or pass them through a potato ricer or a large metal sieve, which will give you a very smooth mash. Beat in the butter and the horseradish sauce and season to taste with salt and pepper. Keep the mash warm over a low heat.

Heat a large skillet until very hot. Add 2 tablespoons of the oil and the hare loins and fry over a high heat, turning now and then, until the meat is nicely browned on all sides. Transfer the loins to a baking sheet, cover with aluminum foil and leave somewhere warm to relax while you cook the spinach. Heat the remaining sunflower oil in the same pan. Add the spinach and stir-fry over a high heat until it has wilted into the bottom of the pan. Tip into a colander and gently press out the excess water. Return the spinach to the pan with the truffle oil, olive oil, and some salt and pepper. Toss for a few seconds over a high heat; then remove from the heat and stir in the chopped truffles, if using.

Carve the loins of hare across into thin slices. Place piles of spinach slightly to one side on 4 warmed plates and overlap the slices of hare on top. Spoon a little of the horseradish mash alongside and serve garnished with some more of the truffle oil drizzled around the edge of the plate.

MEAT

SEARED LAMB'S LIVER
with bubble and squeak cake and shallot gravy

You can make the bubble and squeak cake in advance and reheat it, and the same with the gravy. Lamb's liver is often overlooked in favor of calf's liver but the former is just as tender and tasty as the calf's and half the price! It must be served slightly pink inside, otherwise it becomes tough, dry, and tasteless.

Serves 4

sunflower oil

¼ cup Clarified Butter (see page 183), (optional)

8 thin slices lamb's liver, about 1½ lb (675 g)

4 tablespoons all-purpose flour, seasoned with plenty of Maldon or sea salt and freshly ground white pepper

For the bubble and squeak cake:

1½ lb (675 g) floury potatoes, such as Idaho

1 tablespoon butter

1 large leek, cleaned and thinly sliced

6 oz (175 g) savoy or other green cabbage, roughly chopped

sunflower oil for shallow-frying

For the shallot gravy:

1½ tablespoons sunflower oil

1 onion, chopped

1 carrot, peeled and chopped

2 oz (50 g) mushrooms, sliced

1 fresh bay leaf

1 clove garlic, crushed

1 sprig of fresh thyme

6 white peppercorns, crushed

1¼ cups red or white wine

2½ cups Chicken Stock (see page 181)

1¼ cups Beef Stock (see page 182)

Maldon or sea and freshly ground white pepper

1 tablespoon butter

6 oz (175 g) shallots, peeled and thinly sliced

First make the gravy. You can do this well in advance if you wish. Heat 1 tablespoon of the oil in a large pan. Add the onion, carrot, mushrooms, bay leaf, garlic, thyme, and peppercorns, and fry over a high heat, stirring now and then, until everything is richly golden. Add the wine and boil until it has reduced to a couple of tablespoons. Add the chicken and beef stock and simmer until it has reduced to about 1¼ cups. Strain through a sieve into a clean pan, pressing out as much liquid as you can with the back of a ladle. Taste the gravy and season with salt and more pepper if necessary. Set aside or chill until required.

For the bubble and squeak cake, peel the potatoes and cut them into large chunks. Cook them in boiling salted water for 15–20 minutes until tender. Drain and leave to go cold. Meanwhile, melt the butter in another pan. Add the sliced leek and fry for 4 minutes. Add the cabbage and 2 tablespoons of water; cover and cook over a medium–high heat, giving the pan a good shake every now and then, for 5 minutes. Tip the mixture into a bowl and leave it to go cold. Now crumble the potatoes into the bowl with the cabbage and leek, add plenty of seasoning to taste, and mix together well. If you wish, you can do this ahead and leave all the vegetables to chill in the refrigerator overnight.

Heat a thin layer of oil in an 8 inch (20 cm) heavy-bottomed skillet – it must be flameproof as you will need to slide it into the oven later to finish the cooking. Add the bubble and squeak mixture and press it down well. Leave it to cook over a low heat for about 40 minutes until a good rich crust has formed over the bottom of the cake. Preheat the oven to 350°F (180°C). Slide in the pan and leave to cook for another 30 minutes.

While the bubble and squeak is in the oven, heat the rest of the oil and the butter for the gravy in a small pan. Add the sliced shallots and leave them to cook over a medium heat, stirring them every now and then, until they are soft and richly browned.

Just before you are ready to serve, add the fried shallots to the gravy and leave it over a medium heat to warm through. Heat a large, heavy-bottomed skillet until very hot. Add a little oil, and clarified butter if you wish, to the pan. Coat 2–3 slices of the liver in the seasoned flour. Add to the hot pan and cook for just 1½ minutes on each side, until nicely browned on the outside but still slightly rare in the center. (Don't be tempted to overcrowd the pan.) Lift each lot onto a baking sheet as it cooks and keep it warm while you cook the rest.

To serve, turn the bubble and squeak cake out onto a board, cut it into 4 wedges, and lift them onto 4 warmed serving plates. Place 2 slices of the liver on top of each wedge and spoon the shallot gravy around the edge of the plate.

CASSEROLE OF SPICY MERGUEZ SAUSAGES

with beans, apples, bacon, and cider

Merguez sausages come from North Africa and have a wonderful hot, spicy flavor. Casseroles such as this actually benefit from being made up a day or two before serving as the flavors get time to marry together and improve. This one also freezes well – just leave out the apples and add them to the pot when you reheat it (otherwise they'll turn to mush).

Serves 6

1⅓ cups mixed dried beans, such as navy, red kidney, borlotti, and black-eyed peas

2 lb (900 g) merguez or other spicy sausages

2 tablespoons olive oil

¾ cup bacon lardons (short chunky strips)

1 large onion, thinly sliced

2 cloves garlic, crushed

1¼ cups dry Normandy cider

15 fl oz (450 ml) Chicken Stock (see page 181)

3 fresh bay leaves

3–4 eating apples

1 tablespoon softened butter (optional)

1 tablespoon all-purpose flour (optional)

3 tablespoons chopped fresh parsley

Maldon or sea salt and freshly ground black pepper

The day before you want to serve this dish, cover the beans in lots of cold water and leave them to soak overnight. The next day, bring a pan of water to a boil. Drain the beans; add them to the pan and bring them back to a boil. Boil them vigorously for 10 minutes and then drain once more and set aside.

Twist the sausages into 3–4 inch (7.5–10 cm) lengths. Heat 2 tablespoons of the oil in a large, heavy-bottomed casserole or saucepan. Add the sausages and fry them, turning them now and then, until they are nicely browned all round. Lift them out, cut into their shorter lengths and set to one side. Add the bacon lardons to the pan and fry for 3–4 minutes until golden brown. Add the onion and continue to fry until it is soft and lightly caramelized. Add the garlic and cook for 1 minute. Add the beans to the pan with the cider, chicken stock, and the bay leaves; cover with a tight-fitting lid and leave to simmer for 1–1½ hours or until tender.

Quarter the apples, remove the cores, and then peel. Cut them into thick slices, add to the pan with the browned sausages, and cook for another 30 minutes.

Now you will only need to do the next step if your stew seems a little watery – and this will depend on the beans you've used and how fast they have been cooking. Blend the softened butter with the flour until smooth and then stir it into the stew and leave it to simmer gently for 5 minutes. Stir in the parsley and check the seasoning. Serve in large soup bowls with chunks of crusty fresh bread.

GRIDDLED PORK CHOPS

with oven-roasted vegetables and a tapenade dressing

The roast veggies for this dish can be cooked in advance and reheated, and the dressing can be made in advance and heated through at the last minute.

Serves 4

1 teaspoon fennel seeds

2 cloves garlic, crushed

½ cup olive oil

2 teaspoons lemon juice

Maldon or sea salt and freshly ground
white pepper

4 (1 inch) (2.5 cm) thick pork chops

2 small bulbs of Florence fennel

4 carrots, peeled and cut into 8 pieces

2 parsnips, peeled and cut into chunks

8 oz (225 g) small new potatoes, scrubbed
clean if necessary

8 small whole cloves garlic, unpeeled

3 large sprigs of fresh rosemary, broken into
short pieces

For the tapenade dressing:

1 tablespoon tapenade (black olive paste)

¼ cup extra-virgin olive oil

1 tablespoon balsamic vinegar

1 tablespoon chopped fresh sage and
fennel herb

Preheat the oven to 425°F (220°C). Grind the fennel seeds using a mortar and pestle, with the garlic, 2 tablespoons of the olive oil, the lemon juice, and some seasoning to make a coarse paste. Rub over the surface of the pork chops and set aside at room temperature.

Trim the bulbs of fennel but leave the root ends intact. Cut each bulb into wedges through the root so that each wedge stays together in one piece. Put all the vegetables and the unpeeled cloves of garlic into a roasting pan with the rest of the olive oil and plenty of seasoning. Toss well and then spread into an even layer. Tuck in the pieces of rosemary and roast the vegetables for 45 minutes, turning them every so often as they brown, until they are golden and tender.

Shortly before the vegetables are ready, put the tapenade, olive oil, vinegar, and some seasoning into a small pan. Heat a ridged, cast-iron stove top grill pan over a high heat. Brush it with some oil, add the pork chops, and cook for 4–5 minutes on each side until they are attractively marked in lines and cooked through but still moist and juicy in the center. (There is nothing worse than dry, overcooked pork.) Then tip them on their fatty edges and cook for a couple of minutes until the fat is nice and crisp. Lift them onto a baking sheet and keep warm.

Place the pan of tapenade dressing over a very low heat and leave it to just warm through. Remove the roasted vegetables from the oven and slide the cooked garlic cloves out of their skins. Season with a little more salt and pepper if necessary. Pile the vegetables into the centers of 4 warmed plates and rest a griddled pork chop on top of each pile. Stir the chopped herbs into the dressing and spoon a little around the outside of each plate.

WARM MUTTON SALAD

with olive oil croûtons

Warm salads were much in vogue a couple of years ago, but seem to have fallen out of favor in recent times. This is a bit of a shame as they are relatively quick to throw together, and right up there in the taste league. Mutton is lamb that is more than a year old, and it has a deeper, more mature flavor than a young beast. The down side is that it can be a bit chewy if it isn't hung properly, so make sure you carve it as thinly as possible. Remember to add any juices released during carving to the salad.

Serves 4

4 oz (100 g) baby new potatoes
1 (12 oz) (350 g) fillet of mutton or lamb
Maldon or sea salt and freshly ground
    white pepper
4 tablespoons olive oil
1 tablespoon good-quality balsamic vinegar
1 head frisée lettuce, washed and separated
    into small tendrils
1 red or yellow bell pepper, seeded, finely diced

Tomatoes Concassées (see page 184),
    use 2 tomatoes
1 carrot, peeled and grated
¼ cup pitted black olives
¼ cup Parmesan shavings
small bunch of fresh chives, cut into 2 inch
    (5 cm) lengths

For the croûtons:

½ loaf stale French bread
2 tablespoons olive oil
1 clove garlic, crushed

First cook the potatoes in boiling salted water for 10–15 minutes until just tender. Drain and leave to cool. Then make the croûtons. Tear the bread into small, bite-sized chunks. Heat a heavy-bottomed skillet until quite hot. Add the oil, garlic, and bread, and toss over a high heat for about 5 minutes until crisp and golden brown. Remove the croûtons from the pan and drain on paper towels. Keep them warm. Slice the cooked potatoes and add them to the same pan with a drizzle more oil, if needed. Fry until brown and crispy on both sides. Set aside with the croûtons.

Season the mutton or lamb fillet with salt and pepper. Heat the skillet until very hot. Add 2 tablespoons of oil and the mutton or lamb and sear on each side for about 2 minutes. Take the pan off the heat, lift the meat onto a plate, and set aside to relax in a warm place for a few minutes.

Return the pan to the heat and deglaze with the vinegar, making sure that you scrape up all the crusty bits from the bottom of the pan. Add the remaining oil and season to taste with salt and pepper. Put the lettuce, pepper, tomatoes, carrot, and olives together in a bowl; toss and season. Carve the mutton or lamb into thin slices across the length of the loin. Add the slices to the salad and then pour over the juices from the pan. Add the potatoes, toss once more, and divide between 4 plates. Sprinkle over the croûtons and garnish with the Parmesan and chives.

SCOTTISH ALE-BRAISED OXTAIL

with lima beans

This rustic stew is cooked over a two-day period, which gives time for the meat to become unbelievably tender and enables you to get rid of all the excess fat from the sauce before adding the vegetables and beans. It is nice served in a large tureen. All you need is a big bowl of mash to go with it – and more beer!

Serves 6

2 oxtails, together weighing about 4½ lb (2 kg), cut into 2 inch (5 cm) pieces

6 tablespoons flour with 1 teaspoon Maldon or sea salt and plenty of freshly ground black pepper

4 tablespoons olive oil

1 large onion, chopped

2½ cups Scottish dark ale (or Irish stout)

2 cups Beef Stock (see page 182)

3 cloves garlic, crushed

1 bouquet garni of fresh bay leaves and thyme

Maldon or sea salt and freshly ground black pepper

12 oz (350 g) pearl onions

¼ cup butter

4 stalks celery, sliced

12 oz (350 g) carrots, peeled and sliced

2 (14 oz) (400 g) cans lima beans or other white beans, drained and rinsed

1 clove garlic, very finely chopped

2 tablespoons fresh white breadcrumbs

2 tablespoons chopped fresh flat-leaf parsley

Trim any excess fat off the oxtail and toss it in the seasoned flour. Heat 2 tablespoons of the oil in a large, flameproof casserole. Fry the oxtail a few pieces at a time on all sides until richly browned. Remove to a plate and set aside.

Add another tablespoon of oil to the casserole with the onion and cook over a medium heat, stirring now and then, for 10 minutes or until soft and nicely browned. Stir in any leftover seasoned flour and cook for 1 minute. Take the pan off the heat and gradually stir in the ale and beef stock. Return the oxtail to the pan with the crushed garlic and the bouquet garni; season with a little salt and pepper, cover and simmer for 3 hours, turning the pieces of oxtail over from time to time. Now cover loosely, leave to cool and then refrigerate overnight.

The next day lift the layer of fat off the top of the casserole and discard. Place the oxtail over a gentle heat and bring slowly up to a boil. Meanwhile, fry the button onions in the remaining oil until well browned. Add half the butter, the celery, and carrots, and fry for 3 minutes. Add these vegetables and the lima beans to the casserole and simmer, uncovered, for about 30 minutes, by which time the oxtail and the vegetables should be tender. Remove the bouquet garni.

Heat the rest of the butter in a clean skillet. Add the garlic and the breadcrumbs and fry, stirring continuously, until they are crisp and golden brown. Take the pan off the heat and stir in the parsley and some seasoning. Sprinkle the crumbs over the surface of the oxtail and serve.

TWICE-COOKED SOY-BRAISED PORK

with stir-fried Chinese leaves and steamed rice

The "twice-cooked" refers to the pork first being simmered for a long, slow cook to make it really tender and so that it absorbs all the added flavors. The second cooking is hot and fast to crisp up the fat and give the meat a crispy crust. Plain steamed rice is all this dish needs as an accompaniment as there's so much flavor in the meat and the sauce.

Serves 4

2 lb (900 g) unskinned, boned belly pork in
    one piece
⅔ cup dark soy sauce, plus
    2 tablespoons for sauce
⅔ cup dry sherry
1 long, thin red chili pepper, halved
4 cloves garlic
2½ inch (6 cm) piece ginger root, peeled
    and sliced
2 star anise
sunflower oil for frying

1½ tablespoons hoisin sauce
1 teaspoon sugar
1¾ cup long-grain rice
a pinch of Maldon or sea salt
4 green onions, cut into long, thin shreds

For the stir-fried Chinese leaves:
1 lb (450 g) Peking (Nappa) cabbage leaves
2 tablespoons sunflower oil
1 inch (2.5 cm) piece ginger root, peeled and
    finely chopped
1 long, thin red chili pepper, seeded and very
    finely chopped

Bring 4 pints (2.25 litres) of water to a boil in a large pan. Add the piece of belly pork, ⅔ cup soy sauce, the sherry, red chili pepper, 2 cloves of garlic, two-thirds of the sliced ginger root, and the star anise. Bring back to a boil and leave to simmer very gently for about 2 hours until the pork is meltingly tender.

Remove the pork from the pan to a plate and leave to cool. Strain the stock, reserving ⅔ cup for the sauce. The rest can either be saved for soup or frozen.

For the sauce, very finely chop the remaining ginger and garlic. Heat ½ tablespoon of sunflower oil in a small pan. Add the ginger and garlic, and stir-fry until lightly golden. Add the reserved stock, the 2 tablespoons soy sauce, the hoisin sauce, and the sugar; leave to simmer until reduced and well flavored. Keep the sauce warm.

Rinse the rice under cold water until the water runs clear. Put the rice into a pan with 2½ cups water and the salt. Bring to a boil and boil for 1 minute. Cover and leave to simmer gently for 10 minutes. Then take the pan off the heat, with the lid in place, and leave to steam undisturbed for another 10 minutes.

Meanwhile, pour about 1 inch (2.5 cm) of sunflower oil into a large pan and heat it to 350°F (180°C). While it is coming up to temperature, cut the piece of pork into 4 neat, squared-off pieces and dry them well on paper towels. Also, cut the cabbage leaves into 1 inch (2.5 cm) wide strips. Deep-fry the pieces of pork for 4 minutes until crisp and golden – take care, because as the skin crisps up, the fat tends to spit quite a lot. The bigger and deeper the pan you can use, the better. Drain the pork on paper towels; then slide into a warm oven on a baking sheet to keep crisp.

Now cook the cabbage leaves. Heat the oil in a wok or another large pan. Add the ginger and red chili pepper and stir-fry for a few seconds. Add the cabbage leaves and stir-fry for 2–3 minutes.

Cut each piece of pork across into ¼ inch (5 mm) thick slices. Spoon some steamed rice slightly to one side on 4 plates and arrange overlapping slices of the pork on the outermost sides of the rice. Pile the stir-fried cabbage leaves on the other side of the plates. Skim any fat off the surface of the sauce and spoon the sauce around the edge of each plate. Serve, garnished with the shredded green onions.

ROAST MARINATED LOIN OF LAMB

with basil potatoes

A perfect example of the motto "the simpler the better." If you are lucky enough to get your hands on some good, native new season's lamb, then this recipe is all you need for a truly tasty dish. No fancy sauces or garnishes needed here, just a nice piece of perfectly cooked marinated meat and some new potatoes in buttery basil juices. The meat needs to be marinated a couple of days in advance for maximum flavor and, to finish it off, all you have to do is fling it in the skillet for a few minutes.

Serves 4

5 tablespoons olive oil
2 cloves garlic, crushed
leaves from 2 sprigs of fresh rosemary
1 lb (450g) loin of lamb, trimmed but with the
    skin still on

freshly ground black pepper
1 lb (450 g) new potatoes
Maldon or sea salt
½ cup fresh basil leaves
¼ cup butter

Put 3 tablespoons of the olive oil, the garlic, and the rosemary leaves into a small dish, just large enough to take the lamb. Add the loin and season with about 12 turns of the black-pepper mill; then turn it over in the mixture so that it gets well coated. Cover and set aside to marinate for 4–5 hours at room temperature or, better still, for 12–36 hours in the refrigerator, giving the loin a turn every now and then in the marinade.

When you are ready, cook the potatoes in boiling salted water for 20–25 minutes until tender. Meanwhile, lift the lamb out of the marinade and pick off any bits of garlic and rosemary as they will burn. Season the meat with salt. Heat a skillet until it is very hot. Add the lamb and the rest of the oil and cook for 3 minutes on each side until the meat is nicely browned on the outside but still pink in the center. Remove the pan from the heat and set it aside somewhere warm for 10 minutes to let the meat relax.

Finely chop the basil. Drain the potatoes and return them to the pan with the butter, basil, and a pinch of salt and pepper. Toss together well. Carve the lamb across into thin slices. Divide the potatoes between 4 warmed plates and place some of the lamb on top. Spoon the buttery juices left in the potato pan around the edges of the plates and serve.

SPICED LAMB BALLS

Grinding the lamb lets you use a cheaper cut, such as foreleg or neck, as well as allowing the spices to permeate the meat. Cooking the ground lamb in the tomato sauce ensures a real exchange of tastes between the meat and the sauce. This is the kind of dish which improves by being made ahead so that the flavor matures and intensifies, making it an easy and ideal dish for a dinner party. Simply reheat it before plonking it down on the table in a nice casserole and serving it with plain boiled rice, pasta, or new potatoes. A crisp green salad wouldn't go amiss either.

Serves 4

4 cups ground lamb

2 cloves garlic, crushed

1 tablespoon Worcestershire sauce

2 tablespoons chopped fresh oregano

2 teaspoons ground cumin

1 long, thin red chili pepper, finely diced
   (seeds and all if you like the heat)

4 tablespoons chopped fresh flat-leaf parsley

1 medium farm-fresh egg

Maldon or sea salt and freshly ground
   black pepper

2 tablespoons olive oil

For the tomato and eggplant sauce:

1 medium onion, finely chopped

1 clove garlic, crushed

3 tablespoons olive oil

1 long, thin red chili pepper, finely chopped

1 eggplant, cut into ½ inch (1 cm) dice

1 (14 oz) (400 g) can chopped tomatoes

2 tablespoons tomato ketchup

2 tablespoons chopped fresh basil

For the meatballs, put all the ingredients except the oil in a bowl and season with 1 teaspoon of salt and 20 turns of the black-pepper mill. Mix together well and then shape into balls slightly larger than golfballs. Heat the oil in a large pan. Add the balls (in batches, if necessary, because you want them to brown nicely) and fry them until they are well colored all over. Lift them onto a baking sheet and set aside.

For the sauce, add the onion and garlic to the pan and fry for 5–7 minutes until soft. Add the rest of the oil, the chili pepper, and the diced eggplant (it will absorb lots of oil while cooking) and fry until soft and starting to brown. Now add the tomatoes, ketchup, and some seasoning, and leave the sauce to simmer gently for 20 minutes.

Add the meatballs to the sauce and simmer for another 15 minutes. Stir in the basil and season to taste with salt and pepper. Serve with pasta or plain boiled rice.

VEGETARIAN

CHEESE AND TOMATO SALSA TORTILLAS
with sour cream and salad

In Mexico they fill tortillas (very thin, round, unleavened breads) with almost anything – meat sauces, strips of chicken, refried beans, cheese... Here I have deep-fried some Italian mozzarella cheese in a crispy coating, then rolled it up inside the breads with some sour cream and chili salsa to make a very tasty and substantial lunch or supper dish. If you can't be bothered to make the tortillas – although homemade ones are very easy and much flakier and tastier than store-bought ones – you can buy them from the supermarket instead. But make sure you buy flour tortillas and not those brittle, bright yellow, U-shaped corn ones.

Serves 6

sunflower oil for deep-frying
12 oz (350 g) mozzarella (about 3 balls)
Maldon or sea salt and freshly ground
    black pepper
3 tablespoons all-purpose flour
2 medium farm-fresh eggs, beaten
1½ cups fresh white breadcrumbs
⅔ cup sour cream
4 oz (100 g) mixed baby salad leaves
3 teaspoons extra-virgin olive oil
1 teaspoon lime juice

For the tortillas:

3 cups all-purpose flour
1½ teaspoons Maldon or sea salt
5 tablespoons lard or white vegetable fat
¾ cup warm water

For the tomato salsa:

8 tomatoes, peeled, seeded, and diced
1 red onion, finely chopped
2 green chili peppers, seeded and chopped
juice of 1 lime
3 tablespoons chopped fresh cilantro

For the tortillas, sift the flour and salt into a bowl. Add the fat and rub together into very fine crumbs. Slowly pour in enough warm water, stirring with a small spatula, to make a soft dough. Work it together into a ball with your hands; then transfer it to a lightly floured surface and knead for 3 minutes until smooth. Rub the ball of dough lightly with flour, slip it into a plastic bag and seal. Leave to rest for 1 hour.

Knead the dough once more for a minute and then leave it to rest for another 10 minutes.

Pinch off 12 equal-size pieces of the dough; roll them into neat balls and then flatten them slightly with the palm of your hand. (You should have enough for 12 tortillas.) Dust the work surface, the top of the dough, and the rolling pin with flour; then roll out each flattened ball very thinly into a 7 inch (18 cm) round, dusting everything with a little more flour now and then to prevent sticking.

Heat a smooth, cast-iron griddle or heavy-bottomed skillet over a high heat until very hot. Add a tortilla and cook it for 20 seconds on one side. Flip it over and cook for another 10 seconds; then continue to turn it every 10 seconds until the dough is cooked through and the tortilla is covered on both sides with golden-brown spots. This should take a total of about 1 minute. Repeat with the rest of the tortillas; stack them on a plate and leave them to cool. Divide them into stacks, wrap them in aluminum foil, and reheat them in a warm oven for a couple of minutes just before you are ready to serve.

Mix together all the ingredients for the salsa and set aside. Pour some oil into a large pan so that it is about one-third full and heat it to 375°F (190°C). Cut the mozzarella into ½ × 2½ inch (1 × 6 cm) fingers and dry them off on some paper towels. Season them with a little salt and then dip them first into the flour, then the beaten eggs and finally the breadcrumbs. Deep-fry a few pieces at a time for 1–1½ minutes until crisp and golden brown. Lift out with a slotted spoon onto a baking sheet lined with paper towels and leave to drain for a minute.

To serve, spoon some of the tomato salsa down the center of each tortilla and top with some of the deep-fried cheese. Spoon over a little of the sour cream; roll up and place 2 side by side on 4 serving plates. Toss the salad leaves with the oil, lime juice, and a little seasoning. Pile them in the center of the tortillas and serve.

RÖSTI

with spinach, poached farm eggs, and mustard hollandaise

Very simple, very eggy, very good. As with all straightforward dishes the raw ingredients are of prime importance and this means good baking spuds, preferably Idaho or other potatoes with a high potato mass (which makes them feel heavy) and low sugar content. The spinach should have thick leaves with the biggest stalks removed – tedious I know, but worth it. That leaves the eggs, which make this dish sing. What we need here are farm eggs, *real* free-range eggs from a proper farm, not the so-called free-range eggs from factory farms where the chickens only get to glimpse daylight every now and then. So make an effort to find a farm which has a few chickens grubbing about in the yard and pay good cash for a real treat. If you can get them, not only do they taste sublime (with deeply colored, almost orange, yolks) but they keep their shape much better when poached.

Serves 4

1 tablespoon sunflower oil

1 lb (450 g) fresh leaf spinach, washed and drained

1 tablespoon butter

Maldon or sea salt and freshly ground white pepper

4 farm-fresh eggs

coarsely crushed black peppercorns, to garnish

For the rosti potatoes:

2 (8 oz) (225 g) potatoes, such as Idaho

4 teaspoons olive oil

¼ cup Clarified Butter (see page 183)

For the mustard hollandaise:

¾ cup butter

3 medium farm-fresh egg yolks

1 teaspoon Dijon mustard

First make the rösti potatoes. Peel and coarsely grate the potatoes into a bowl. Season with ½ teaspoon of salt and some pepper. Heat half the oil and half the butter in one 8 inch (20 cm) heavy-bottomed skillet or 4 individual 5 inch (12.5 cm) blini pans. Add the potato mix and press it down evenly with the back of a spatula. Fry over a low–medium heat for about 15 minutes until you can see traces of color at the edges – but take care not to cook it over too high a heat or it will over-brown before the potato on the inside has had a chance to cook. Cover the pan(s) with an inverted plate, hold the two together, and turn over so that the rösti is transferred to the plate. Heat the remaining oil and butter in the pan. Slide the rösti back in on its uncooked side and cook for another 10–15 minutes until golden. Now you can either keep the rösti warm, or leave to cool and reheat later in the oven at 350°F (180°C) for 5 minutes.

For the mustard hollandaise, melt the butter in a small pan and keep it hot. Put the yolks and mustard into a large, heatproof bowl; add 1 tablespoon of hot water and rest the bowl over a pan of barely simmering water. Whisk for 3–4 minutes until the mixture becomes pale, thick, and moussey. Then gradually whisk in the butter, a tablespoon at a time, taking care not to let the mixture get too hot or it will curdle. Take the bowl off the heat and whisk in a couple of pinches of salt and 8 turns of the pepper mill. Keep the sauce warm while you cook the eggs and the spinach – a clever trick is to fill a thermos with hot water, drain it, and dry it well. Pour in the hollandaise and seal the flask. It will keep warm for ages.

For the spinach, heat the oil in a large pan; add the spinach and stir-fry over a high heat until it wilts into the bottom. Tip it into a colander and gently press out the excess liquid; then return it to the pan and toss with the butter and some seasoning. Keep it warm.

To poach the eggs, pour 1½ inches (3.5 cm) of boiling water into a clean skillet and place it over a low heat – the water should show a few bubbles on the bottom of the pan, but no more. Break the eggs carefully into the hot water and cook for 3 minutes, basting the tops of the eggs with a little of the hot water as they cook. Lift them out of the water with a slotted spoon and drain on paper towels.

To serve, cut the large potato rösti into quarters and lift one piece onto each plate, or place the individual röstis in the centers of 4 plates. Spoon on some of the spinach, add a poached egg, and then spoon over some of the hollandaise. Sprinkle with a·little of the coarsely crushed black peppercorns and serve immediately.

BAKED GNOCCHI

with wild mushrooms, garlic, and Parmesan

This really proves that you don't need to have meat with every meal. Without the mushrooms, this dish is known as gnocchi alla romana and is essentially a thick mixture of Parmesan-flavored polenta, set in a baking sheet, and then cut into pieces and baked in the oven until crisp and golden. Layered with a mixture of wild mushrooms and topped with a crisp crust of more cheese and breadcrumbs, it turns into something that even the meat-eaters will fight over.

Serves 4

4¼ cups water
1¾ cups quick-cook polenta (cornmeal)
½ cup finely grated Parmesan
1 farm-fresh egg yolk
a pinch of freshly grated nutmeg
2 tablespoons melted butter

Maldon or sea salt
3 tablespoons olive oil
1 lb (450 g) mixed wild mushrooms, wiped
   clean and hard stalks removed
2 cloves garlic, crushed
1 tablespoon fresh white breadcrumbs
1 tablespoon chopped fresh parsley

Bring the water to a boil in a large pan. Reduce the heat and then slowly whisk in the polenta, making sure that you don't get any lumps. Leave it to cook over a very low heat for 10 minutes, whisking it frequently, until it becomes thick and comes away from the sides of the pan. Take the pan off the heat and stir in 3 tablespoons of the Parmesan, the egg yolk, nutmeg, 1 tablespoon of the melted butter, and salt to taste. Pour the mixture into a lightly greased 9 × 13 inch (23 × 33 cm) jelly roll pan and spread it out with a wet spatula so that the mixture is level and no more than ½ inch (1 cm) thick. Cover and chill for at least 2 hours or overnight.

Preheat the oven to 400°F (200°C). Cut the polenta mixture into 24 small squares and set to one side. Heat the oil in a large, deep skillet. Cut the mushrooms where necessary into thick slices; add to the pan with the garlic and fry over a high heat for about 3 minutes.

Arrange overlapping squares of the gnocchi and mushrooms in lines in a well-buttered 8 × 11 inch (20 × 28 cm) shallow, ovenproof dish. Mix the rest of the melted butter with the breadcrumbs and stir in the rest of the Parmesan and the tablespoon of chopped parsley. Sprinkle over the top of the dish and bake in the oven for 25–30 minutes until crisp and golden. Serve immediately.

STICKY RICE TEMPURA

with avocado and mango salsa, herb salad, and soy vinaigrette

This takes the sushi rice idea one step farther by enclosing it in a crispy tempura batter and serving it with a salsa on top and a few dressed leaves. Make up the salsa in advance (without the cilantro), then make the rice patties and deep-fry them at the last moment.

Serves 6

Scant 2 cups Japanese sticky rice
2½ cups water
2 tablespoons superfine sugar
1 teaspoon Maldon or sea salt
4 tablespoons rice vinegar
sunflower oil for deep-frying
1 teaspoon wasabi paste

For the avocado and mango salsa:

1 ripe but firm mango
1 ripe but firm avocado
1 small red onion, finely diced
1 long, thin red chili pepper, finely diced
  (seeds and all if you like the heat)
finely grated zest and juice of 1 lime
2 tablespoons Japanese pickled ginger,
  drained and cut into fine shreds
2 tablespoons olive oil
½ teaspoon Maldon or sea salt
freshly ground white pepper
4 tablespoons chopped fresh cilantro

For the soy vinaigrette:

2 tablespoons good-quality soy sauce
⅔ cup best-quality olive oil
1 teaspoon Dijon mustard
2 tablespoons lime juice
1 teaspoon clear honey

For the tempura batter:

5 tablespoons self-rising flour
6 tablespoons cornstarch
ice-cold sparkling mineral water

For the herb salad:

a handful of mixed cilantro, chervil, and
  chive sprigs
a few drops of olive oil
½ teaspoon lime juice

For the sticky rice tempura, put the rice into a sieve and wash it under running cold water, working your fingers through the grains until the water runs clear. Drain the rice and put it into a pan with the water. Bring it quickly to a boil; then the heat turn down very low and cook for 10 minutes. Remove from the heat, cover and leave undisturbed for 10 minutes. This timing is crucial to produce the correct consistency for the sticky rice.

Stir the sugar and salt into the vinegar until dissolved. Turn the rice out into a bowl and stir

in the vinegar mixture, fanning the rice as you do so to cool it and produce a sheen on it. Divide the rice mixture into 6 and shape into small 4 inch (10 cm) patties. Cover and leave in the refrigerator for 2 hours to set.

For the avocado and mango salsa, peel the mango and then slice the flesh away from either side of the flat pit in 2 whole pieces. Cut into small, neat dice. Cut the avocado in half and remove the pit. You can do this by whacking the pit with a sharp knife so that the blade grips it. Give a gentle twist and the pit will come out very easily. Cut the avocado into quarters and peel off the skin; cut the flesh into small dice the same size as the mango. Mix in a bowl with the rest of the salsa ingredients, cover and leave to marinate at room temperature for at least 1 hour.

Meanwhile, make the soy vinaigrette. Simply whisk all the ingredients together and set aside until you are ready to serve.

Shortly before serving, pour some sunflower oil into a pan until it is about one-third full and heat it to 350°F (180°C). Smear one side of each rice cake with some of the wasabi paste. Make the tempura batter by sifting the flour and cornstarch into a bowl. Mix in enough sparkling mineral water (make sure it is ice-cold) with a fork to make a slightly lumpy batter with the consistency of light cream. Dip the rice cakes in the batter and fry 2 at a time until crisp and lightly golden – about 4 minutes. Lift them out with a slotted spoon onto some paper towels and leave to drain while you cook the rest.

Place a rice cake in the center of a plate. Spoon some of the salsa into a 2 inch (5 cm) plain pastry cutter and press down lightly. Using a fish slice or a spatula, carefully lift the salsa onto the center of the rice cake and remove the cutter. Repeat for the rest of the cakes. For the herb salad, toss the herb sprigs with the oil and lime juice and pile on top. Put the soy vinaigrette in a small bowl and serve separately.

EGGPLANT FRITTER STACKS

with crème fraîche raita and curry oil

The combination of these crispy eggplant wafers and the fresh and spicy tomato sauce, flecked with cilantro, makes a delicious vegetarian starter too.

Serves 4

2 medium eggplants, peeled and
　　coarsely grated
Maldon or sea salt and freshly ground
　　black pepper
1 ⅓ cups chickpea flour
1 tablespoon ground coriander
2 teaspoons ground cumin
½ teaspoon turmeric powder
½ teaspoon cayenne pepper
1 tablespoon sunflower oil, plus extra for
　　shallow frying
1½ tablespoons lemon juice
¾ cup warm water
2 medium farm-fresh egg whites

1 recipe Crème Fraîche Raita (see page 50)
a little Curry Oil (see page 187), to serve

For the tomato sauce:

2 tablespoons olive oil
1 medium onion, very finely chopped
1 large clove garlic, crushed
1 long, thin red chili pepper, finely chopped,
　　seeds and all
1 (14 oz) (400 g) can chopped tomatoes
2 tablespoons tomato ketchup
1 sprig of fresh thyme
1 fresh bay leaf
2 tablespoons chopped fresh cilantro
Maldon or sea salt and freshly ground
　　black pepper

Mix the eggplants with 1 teaspoon of salt and set aside in a sieve to drain. Sift the chickpea flour, spices, and 1 teaspoon of salt together into a bowl. Make a well and add 1 tablespoon sunflower oil, the lemon juice, and water; stir together. Beat well with an electric whisk to make a smooth batter and set aside for 30 minutes. Meanwhile, make the tomato sauce. Heat the oil in a pan. Add the onion, garlic, and chili and fry for 5 minutes until soft but not colored. Add the tomatoes, ketchup, thyme, and bay leaf, and leave to simmer for 30 minutes until quite thick.

Rinse the eggplants under cold water to remove the excess salt and then squeeze well, first in your hands and then in a clean dish towel. Stir them into the batter. Whisk the egg whites with a pinch of salt into soft peaks and gently fold the egg whites into the batter. Pour about ½ inch (1 cm) of sunflower oil into a large skillet. Drop in large spoonfuls of the eggplant batter, spacing them a little apart, and fry for 3–4 minutes on each side over a medium heat until golden. Drain on paper towels and keep warm while you cook the rest. You should have 12 fritters in total.

To serve, stir the cilantro into the sauce and season to taste with salt and pepper. Place one fritter in the center of a warmed plate and cover with a spoonful of the sauce. Cover with another fritter, some more sauce, and then a third fritter. Pile the crème fraîche raita on top of the last fritter and drizzle a little curry oil around the edge of the plate.

CHANTERELLE MUSHROOM RISOTTO

with Parmesan and flat-leaf parsley

There is something very special about the flavor of chanterelle mushrooms. They have a heavenly apricot perfume, especially when freshly picked, and if you've been scouring the forests for these yellow beauties, this recipe is as good a use for them as you'll find. If you're buying them from a store (and I have seen them in a British supermarket recently), then make sure that they are pale yellow to golden, with no brown soggy bits. They should have a firm texture and should, when sliced, be almost white inside. They're in season in Britain from late June until the end of October.

Serves 4

1 lb (450 g) chanterelle mushrooms
½ cup olive oil
5 tablespoons butter
8 oz (225 g) shallots, finely chopped
1¼ cps arborio rice
1 cup dry white wine

3¾ cups Chicken Stock
  (see page 181)
¼ cup finely grated Parmesan
3 tablespoons coarsely chopped fresh flat-leaf
  parsley, plus extra for garnishing
Maldon or sea salt and freshly ground
  black pepper
slivers of Parmesan, to garnish

Brush any dirt off the mushrooms with a dry pastry brush and then wipe them clean with a damp cloth. Heat 2 tablespoons of the oil and 2 tablespoons of the butter in a large, heavy-bottomed pan. Add the mushrooms and fry over a high heat for 2–3 minutes until they are nicely colored. Tip them onto a plate and set aside.

Add the rest of the oil and the shallots to the pan and cook over a medium heat until the shallots are soft and lightly browned. Add the rice and stir it around for about a minute until all the grains are coated in the oil.

Add the white wine to the pan and simmer quite vigorously until it has almost disappeared. Then add 1¼ cups of the stock and continue to cook over a gentle heat, stirring until it has all been absorbed by the rice. Continue to cook, adding the stock 1¼ cups at a time, until it has all been absorbed and the rice is tender and creamy, but still with a little bit of bite left in it. This should take about 20 minutes in total.

Stir in the rest of the butter, the grated Parmesan, chopped parsley, chanterelles, and salt and pepper to taste. Warm through, then remove from the heat.

Spoon the mixture into 4 warmed bowls and sprinkle with the Parmesan slivers and a little more chopped parsley. Serve with a hunk of whole wheat bread if you wish.

Whisky – the jewel in Scotland's crown, the "water of life" – is not just the world's best-known spirit. For me its complex, sometimes exotic, flavors are an inspiration for some of my favorite desserts.

DESSERTS

THREE-CHOCOLATE MARQUISE

with crème fraîche sorbet

This is a bit of a restaurant dessert and requires a fair bit of time and effort, but you will be rewarded with a very sexy pudding. The crème fraîche sorbet gives just the right amount of acidity to balance the richness of the chocolate. The sorbet also works well made with mascarpone instead of crème fraîche. And it has to be said that the marquise also tastes great made with only one type of chocolate, so it then needs to be called One-Chocolate Marquise.

In the restaurant we use sheets of leaf gelatin to set this terrine but this is not very easy to come by. Do use it instead of the powdered variety, though, if you're lucky enough to find some. You just need to soak the leaves in plenty of cold water for a few minutes, then lift them out and add them to the bowl of chocolate when you are melting it.

Serves 12

2 cups milk

8 medium farm-fresh egg yolks

5 tablespoons superfine sugar

2 cups heavy cream

7 squares milk chocolate, broken into
    small pieces

7 squares white chocolate, broken into
    small pieces

7 squares dark chocolate, broken into
    small pieces

4 (¼ oz) (10 g) envelopes unflavored
    powdered gelatin plus 1 teaspoon, or
16 × 3 g sheets of leaf gelatin

For the crème fraîche sorbet:

1¼ cups superfine sugar

1½ cups water

2 tablespoons strained fresh orange juice

1 lb 2 oz (500 g) crème fraîche

Pour the milk into a pan and bring it up to a boil. Meanwhile, cream the egg yolks with the sugar until pale and creamy. Just before the milk is about to boil over the sides of the pan, whisk it into the egg yolks. Return the mixture to the pan and cook over a gentle heat for a couple of minutes, stirring, until it lightly coats the back of a wooden spoon. Stir in the heavy cream. Divide the mixture equally between 3 bowls and leave it to cool.

Place the milk chocolate in a heatproof bowl and bring about 1 inch (2.5 cm) of water up to a simmer in a pan. Rest the bowl of milk chocolate over the pan and leave it to melt. Add 2 sheets of the soaked leaf gelatin, if using, to the bowl. If using powdered gelatin, put 4½ tablespoons of cold water into a small pan and sprinkle over 4½ teaspoons of the gelatin; leave it to "sponge" for 5 minutes. Melt it over a low heat until clear. Stir the dissolved gelatin and then the melted milk chocolate into one bowl of the custard and mix together well until smooth. Line a 3 inch (7.5 cm) deep, 3 × 10 inch (7.5 × 25 cm) Le Creuset or similar terrine dish with plastic wrap so that it overhangs the sides and is tucked down well into the corners. Pour in the milk chocolate custard and leave it to chill in the refrigerator until set.

Now repeat this procedure with the white chocolate but use another 2 sheets of soaked leaf gelatin, or 5 teaspoons of powdered gelatin and 5 tablespoons of cold water. Pour this on top of the milk chocolate layer and leave it to set. Finally repeat once more using the dark chocolate, the remaining soaked leaf gelatin or 4 teaspoons of powdered gelatin and 4 tablespoons of cold water. Pour into the terrine dish and leave to set. Then cover the whole terrine with the overhanging plastic wrap and leave it until you are ready to serve.

For the crème fraîche sorbet, put the sugar and water into a medium-size pan and place over a high heat. Bring to a boil, stirring from time to time. Leave the syrup to simmer for 5 minutes, skimming off any impurities as they rise to the surface. Remove it from the heat and leave it to cool; then whisk in the orange juice and crème fraîche and chill the mixture in the refrigerator for a few hours until it is really cold.

Now you can either churn the mixture in an ice cream machine or pour it into a plastic box and freeze until almost firm. If doing the latter, scrape the mixture into a food processor and whizz until smooth. Pour it back into the box and repeat one more time. Return the sorbet to the freezer and freeze until firm.

To serve, invert the marquise onto a board, cut it into ½ inch (1 cm) slices and serve with an oval of the crème fraîche sorbet.

Tarte Tatins

Four variations on the classic apple tarte tatin, each with its own accompaniment. Either make one big tart or little individual ones using 5 inch (12.5 cm) blini pans. These aren't as difficult as you may think, and work just fine with bought puff pastry.

BANANA TARTE TATIN

with rum cream

The love affair between the flavors of banana and rum has always been intense; they belong together, especially in a dish like this where the bananas are glossy with sticky-sweet caramelized juices and the rum is infused in cool, freshly whipped cream.

Serves 6

5 tablespoons superfine sugar
¼ cup unsalted butter
4 large bananas
12 oz (350 g) puff pastry
flour, for rolling out pastry

For the rum cream:

1 tablespoon light brown sugar
2 tablespoons dark rum or to taste
1¼ cups whipping cream
a pinch of cinnamon, to decorate

Preheat the oven to 375°F (190°C). If making one large tart, put the sugar and butter into a flameproof 10 inch (25 cm) cast-iron skillet. If making smaller tarts, divide the sugar and butter evenly between six 5 inch (12.5 cm) blini pans. Cook over a medium heat, stirring now and then, until the mixture turns into a smooth toffee. It will look very grainy to start with and the butter will look as if it has split away from the sugar, but just keep stirring and it will gradually come together. Now take the pan(s) off the heat and make sure that the toffee covers the base in an even layer.

Peel the bananas and cut them sharply on the diagonal into long thick slices. Arrange them randomly over the bottom of the pan(s), overlapping them here and there, so that they cover the toffee in a thick layer. For the large tart, roll out the pastry on a lightly floured surface into a 11 inch (28 cm) round – don't worry about it being too neat. For the individual tarts, divide the pastry into 6 and roll each piece out into a 6 inch (15 cm) round. Lay the pastry over the bananas and tuck the edges down into the pan(s) to make the rim(s) of the tart(s). Prick the top of the pastry here and there with a fork; then slide the pan(s) into the oven and bake for 25 minutes for the smaller tarts, or 30 minutes for the larger one, until risen and golden.

Meanwhile, make the rum cream. Mix the sugar with the rum until the sugar has dissolved. Whip the cream until it begins to show signs of thickening, then whisk in the sweetened rum until it forms soft peaks. Cover and chill until you are ready to serve.

Remove the pan(s) from the oven and leave to rest for 10 minutes. Then run a sharp knife around the pastry to make sure that all the edges are free and place an inverted plate over the top of the pan(s). Turn the two over together and remove the pan(s). Cut the large tart into 6 wedges. Serve with the rum cream, sprinkled with a little cinnamon.

PEAR AND RAISIN TARTE TATIN

with mascarpone cheese

Pears, like apples, have a lovely soft but firm texture that makes for an excellent tarte tatin. Dried raisins add little concentrated bursts of sweetness, and you can experiment by adding other dried fruits, such as apricots or dates.

Serves 6

⅔ cup muscatel raisins

¼ cup Muscat Beaumes de Venise or another sweet dessert wine

5 tablespoons superfine sugar

¼ cup unsalted butter

2 lb (900 g) ripe but firm Bosc pears

12 oz (350 g) puff pastry

flour, for rolling out pastry

7 oz (200 g) mascarpone cheese, to serve

Mix the raisins with the wine, cover and leave to soak overnight. The next day make the toffee in the pan(s) as in the recipe for *Banana Tarte Tatin* on page 132. Halve the pears; scoop out the cores with a melon baller or teaspoon and then peel. If making one large tart, arrange them over the bottom of the pan rounded-side down with their thin tips pointing towards the center. For individual tarts, place 2 pear halves on the bottom of each pan, heel to toe so that they nestle nicely together. Fill the cavity of each one with some of the soaked raisins and scatter the rest into the gaps between each piece of fruit. Cover with the pastry, prick with a fork, and bake for 25–30 minutes.

Depending on the type of pears that you have used, there might be quite a lot of syrupy juices in the bottom of the pan(s). Before you turn out the tart(s), carefully pour these off into a small pan and boil them rapidly until they become thick and toffee-like once more. Turn out the tart(s) and spoon over the toffee. Serve each portion with a good spoonful of mascarpone cheese.

MANGO TARTE TATIN

with crème fraîche

The crème fraîche cuts into the smooth sweetness of the mango in a most delicious way.

Serves 6

5 tablespoons superfine sugar
¼ cup unsalted butter

1 very large or 2 smaller ripe, firm mangoes
12 oz (350 g) puff pastry
flour, for rolling out pastry
Scant 1 cup crème fraîche, to serve

Make the tart(s) in the same way as the *Banana Tarte Tatin* on page 132, using the mangoes instead of the bananas. Peel the mangoes and slice the fruit away from either side of the thin flat pit in 2 whole pieces. Place the slices of fruit cut-side down on a board and slice into long ½ inch (1 cm) thick slices. Then cut away any bits of fruit left on the pit and use them to fill in any gaps. Assemble and bake the tart(s) as before and serve with scoops of crème fraîche instead of the rum cream.

FRESH FIG TARTE TATIN

with fromage blanc

There's something luxurious about fresh figs – I think it's the rich, red-purple color of the flesh. The golden, crisp pastry combined with the soft acidity of fromage blanc makes this a real star dish.

Serves 6

5 tablespoons superfine sugar
¼ cup unsalted butter

8 ripe figs, halved
12 oz (350 g) puff pastry
flour, for rolling out pastry
Scant 1 cup fromage blanc, to serve

Make the tart(s) in the same way as the *Banana Tarte Tatin* on page 132, using the figs instead of the bananas. Serve with fromage blanc (or fromage frais) instead of the rum cream.

HOT PASSION FRUIT SOUFFLÉS

I like to make these little soufflés using 3–4 passion fruit for each one so that you get a really sherbety taste, but you could cut the number of fruit by half and make the "jam" with just 2 tablespoons of superfine sugar if you wish. The usual soufflé rules apply here but for some reason these seem to rise higher than any other soufflé I know.

Serves 6

24 passion fruit
generous ¾ cup superfine sugar, plus extra for dusting and to serve

a little butter for greasing
1½ cups milk
3 medium farm-fresh egg yolks
1½ tablespoons cornstarch
1½ tablespoons all-purpose flour
6 medium farm-fresh egg whites

Cut each passion fruit in half and scoop out the pulp into a small pan. Add ¼ cup of the sugar and stir over a gentle heat until the sugar has dissolved. Bring the mixture to a boil and boil it rapidly for about 10 minutes, stirring frequently toward the end of the cooking, until you are left with a thick "jam." Pass this through a sieve to remove the seeds and set aside.

Slide a baking sheet onto the middle shelf of the oven and preheat it to 400°F (200°C). Lightly butter six 3 inch (7.5 cm) ramekins and dust them out with a little extra sugar.

Pour all but 1 tablespoon of the milk into a pan and slowly bring it to a boil. Meanwhile, beat the egg yolks, 3 tablespoons of the sugar, the cornstarch, flour, and remaining milk together in a bowl until smooth. Whisk in the hot milk, return the mixture to the pan, and bring to a boil, stirring. Reduce the heat and leave the mixture to simmer very gently for about 10 minutes, beating it every now and then, until you have cooked out the taste of the flour.

Pour the custard into a bowl and beat in the passion fruit "jam." Whisk the egg whites into soft peaks and then whisk in the remaining sugar. Lightly whisk one-quarter of the whites into the custard to loosen it slightly, then carefully fold in the remainder. Spoon the mixture into the prepared ramekins; level the tops and then run the tip of a knife around the inside edge of each dish to release the mixture. Slide the ramekins onto the baking sheet and bake for 10–12 minutes until the soufflés are well risen, browned, and doubled in height but still slightly wobbly. Quickly lift them onto small dessert plates and sprinkle with a little more superfine (or confectioners') sugar. Serve straightaway before they've got time to sink.

TUILE OF LEMON CURD ICE CREAM

with strawberry sauce

Instead of making the ice cream, you could stir some good-quality lemon curd into some good vanilla ice cream and freeze it once more until firm. For the strawberry sauce, you need to check out the sweetness of your strawberries and add only enough sugar to taste. The tuiles make great little nests to hold the ice cream and sauce.

Serves 6

For the lemon curd:
2 farm-fresh eggs
finely grated zest and juice of 1 large lemon
5 tablespoons superfine sugar
¼ cup unsalted butter

For the ice cream:
2½ cups milk
6 medium farm-fresh egg yolks
5 tablespoons superfine sugar
1 cup heavy cream

For the tuile baskets:
2 tablespoons superfine sugar
3 tablespoons all-purpose flour
1 medium farm-fresh egg white
2 tablespoons melted butter

For the strawberry sauce:
12 oz (350 g) fresh strawberries, hulled
5 tablespoons superfine sugar or to taste

For the lemon curd, beat the eggs together and then strain them through a sieve into a heatproof bowl. Add the lemon zest and juice, sugar, and butter. Rest the bowl over a pan of barely simmering water and cook, stirring, for about 20 minutes until the mixture is smooth and thickened. Remove the bowl from the pan and leave the curd to cool.

For the ice cream, pour the milk into a pan and slowly bring to a boil. Meanwhile, whisk the egg yolks and sugar together until pale and creamy. Whisk in the hot milk, return the mixture to the pan, and cook over a gentle heat, stirring continuously, until it lightly coats the back of a wooden spoon. Pour into a bowl, leave to cool, and then stir in the cream. Cover and leave in the refrigerator until the mixture is really cold and then stir in the lemon curd. Now you can either churn the mixture in an ice cream machine or pour it into a plastic box and freeze until almost firm. If you are doing the latter, scrape the mixture into a food processor and whizz until smooth. Pour it back into the box and repeat the process once more. Return the ice cream to the freezer and freeze until firm.

For the tuile baskets, put the sugar, flour, and egg white into a bowl and beat together into a smooth paste. Beat in the melted butter and leave the mixture to chill in the refrigerator for 20 minutes. Preheat the oven to 350°F (180°C). Then drop about 3 teaspoons of the mixture well apart onto a lightly greased baking sheet and spread it out very thinly into approximately 5 inch (12.5 cm) rounds. Bake for 6–8 minutes until golden brown around the edges. Remove from the oven and leave to cool for a few seconds; then quickly lift off the baking sheet with a spatula and drape over the bottom of 3 upturned ramekins or small dessert molds. Pleat the cookies into a cup-shape and leave to cool and go crisp. Repeat with the rest of the mixture.

For the strawberry sauce, slice the strawberries into a bowl and stir in the sugar. Leave for a few minutes until they have become juicy. Whizz the mixture in a blender or with a hand blender until smooth and then press through a sieve into a clean bowl. Cover and chill.

To serve, scoop the ice cream into neat balls and drop them into the tuile baskets. Place the baskets on dessert plates and spoon some of the strawberry sauce around them.

CLOOTIE DUMPLING

with clotted cream

A real Scottish dish and none the worse for that, traditionally made in an old pillow case. I recently judged a clootie dumpling competition and I learned that a perfect pudding should be as spherical as possible, have an unblemished shiny coating, and a dense, moist, flavorsome interior. Clotted cream is the perfect accompaniment.

Serves 8

2 cups all-purpose flour, plus 3 tablespoons for sprinkling
1 teaspoon baking soda
1 teaspoon mixed spice
1 teaspoon cinnamon
1 teaspoon ginger
¼ teaspoon Maldon or sea salt
¾ cup superfine sugar, plus 1 tablespoon for sprinkling

½ cup shredded suet
⅔ cup golden raisins
½ cup currants
½ cup chopped, pitted dates
⅓ cup muscatel raisins
1 apple or carrot, coarsely grated
1 tablespoon molasses
1 medium farm-fresh egg
⅔ cup buttermilk
1 cup clotted or heavy cream, to serve

Sift the flour, baking soda, spices, and salt into a bowl. Stir in the sugar, suet, dried fruits, and the grated apple or carrot. Mix the molasses with the egg and some of the buttermilk and mix into the dry ingredients to give a soft mixture with a cake-like dropping consistency.

Dip a large piece of muslin, an old pillow case, or a dish towel into boiling water, then squeeze out the excess water. Lay it out on a surface and sprinkle a 12 inch (30 cm) round in the center with the 3 tablespoons of flour and the tablespoon of sugar. Spoon the dumpling mixture on top; then bring the opposite corners of the cloth together over the top and tie securely with string, leaving a little room for the dumpling to expand.

Rest a large heatproof plate in the bottom of a large pan on some sort of trivet or container so that it is not in direct contact with the heat and place the dumpling on the plate, knotted side up. Pour in enough water almost to cover the dumpling. Cover with a tight-fitting lid and simmer gently for 3¾–4 hours. Every now and then check the water level and top it up if necessary.

Preheat the oven to 350°F (180°C). Lift the dumpling out of the pan and dip it briefly in a bowl of cold water – this will ensure that the outside of the dumpling does not stick to the cloth when you unwrap it. Undo the package, fold back the cloth and invert the dumpling onto an ovenproof serving plate. Slide it into the oven and leave it for about 15 minutes until the outside of the dumpling has dried off. Serve in chunky wedges with scoops of cream and perhaps a small glass of whisky.

FROZEN CHOCOLATE CAKE

with mascarpone

One from my pal Jim Kerr (chef, not singer) who is now the general manager of my new Glasgow restaurant, Nairns. This chocolate cake is very nice and a little goes a long way. The mascarpone helps it slip down a treat. (Note that the mascarpone has raw egg yolk in it, in case that's a problem for you.)

Serves 8

7 squares semisweet chocolate
   (65 percent cocoa solids)
Scant 1 cup superfine sugar
Scant 1 cup unsalted butter
⅔ cup espresso coffee
3 medium farm-fresh eggs

For the mascarpone:
9 oz (250 g) mascarpone cheese
1 tablespoon superfine sugar
1 medium farm-fresh egg yolk

For the frozen chocolate cake, line an 8 × 12 inch (20 × 30 cm) shallow rectangular pan with nonstick baking parchment. Preheat the oven to 350°F (180°C).

Break the chocolate into a pan and add the sugar, butter. and espresso coffee. Leave it over a low heat until everything has melted and then increase the heat slightly and let the mixture come up to a gentle simmer. Leave it to simmer for 10 minutes, stirring frequently, until the mixture has slightly caramelized.

Break the eggs into a bowl and whisk together lightly. Beat in the caramelized chocolate mixture and mix together well. Pour the mixture through a sieve into the prepared pan and bake in the center of the oven for 30 minutes. Remove the cake from the oven and leave it to cool. Then transfer it to the freezer and leave it until it has just frozen, but not so that it is rock hard.

Meanwhile, beat the mascarpone together with the superfine sugar and egg yolk in a bowl until thick. Cover with plastic wrap and chill in the refrigerator.

To serve, remove the cake from the freezer and lift it out of the pan. Peel back the baking parchment and cut the cake in half lengthwise and then across into 4 so that you end up with 8 rectangular pieces. Lift onto dessert plates and serve with ovals of the mascarpone.

OATY RHUBARB CRUMBLES

with rhubarb sauce and crème anglaise

Crumbles have long been a favorite of mine but they do not make very attractive restaurant-style desserts. However, layering up the components in large metal pastry rings solves the problem and the two different sauces make them look stunning.

Serves 6

2 lb (900 g) rhubarb, trimmed
6 slices fresh ginger root
zest of 1 small orange, grated
¾ cup superfine sugar

For the crumble mixture:
2¼ cups all-purpose flour
⅔ cup butter

⅔ cup soft light brown sugar
1 cup rolled oats

For the crème anglaise:
½ vanilla bean
1¼ cups milk
3 medium farm-fresh egg yolks
2 tablespoons superfine sugar

For the crème anglaise, split open the vanilla bean and scrape out all the little black seeds. Put the bean and the seeds into a small pan with the milk and bring to a boil. Remove from the heat and leave to infuse for 20 minutes.

Preheat the oven to 400°F (200°C). Cut the rhubarb into 1 inch (2.5 cm) pieces and place in a pan with the sliced ginger, orange zest, and sugar. Cover and cook over a gentle heat for a few minutes, stirring very gently every now and then, until the rhubarb is only just tender and still holding its shape. Tip the mixture into a sieve set over a small clean pan. Discard the pieces of ginger and orange zest and set the rhubarb aside to let the syrup drain out of it.

Meanwhile, sift the flour into a large bowl and rub in the butter until the mixture looks like fine breadcrumbs. Stir in 2 tablespoons of the sugar. Place six 4 inch (10 cm) lightly buttered metal pastry cutters on a baking sheet and spoon about 2 tablespoons of the flour and butter mixture into the base of each one. Spread out evenly and then press down very lightly with the back of the spoon. Stir the rest of the sugar and the rolled oats into the remaining crumble mixture.

Divide the rhubarb between each ring and level the tops; then cover with a layer of the crumble topping. Bake for 25–30 minutes until crisp and golden. Meanwhile, finish the crème anglaise. Beat the egg yolks and sugar together in a bowl until pale and creamy. Bring the milk back to a boil, lift out the vanilla bean and whisk the hot milk into the egg yolks. Return the mixture to the pan and cook over a gentle heat, stirring continuously, until it lightly coats the back of a wooden spoon. Keep the crème anglaise warm. Gently warm the rhubarb syrup.

To serve, slide a fish slice under each crumble and place in the center of a warmed dessert plate. Carefully lift off the cutters and pour around some of the rhubarb sauce and crème anglaise.

WALNUT AND WHISKY TARTS

with athol brose cream

These are a bit like mini pecan pies but made with walnuts and flavored with Scotch whisky instead of the more classic bourbon. They are definitely for those of you with a sweet tooth, but serve them with plain whipped cream to cut through some of this richness if you prefer.

Serves 6

4½ tablespoons butter
½ cup light brown sugar
2 medium farm-fresh eggs
½ cup light corn syrup
1½ tablespoons whisky
a pinch of salt
generous 1 cup walnut pieces
1½ tablespoons all-purpose flour

6 (4 inch) (10 cm) Sweet Pastry tartlet shells
  (see page 188)
1 cup walnut halves, to decorate

For the athol brose cream:

⅓ cup whipping cream
1½ tablespoons clear honey
  (heather if possible)
¼ cup whisky

Preheat the oven to 350°F (180°C). Beat the butter and brown sugar together until pale and fluffy. Beat in the eggs, one at a time, and then slowly mix in the corn syrup, whisky, and salt. Mix the walnut pieces with the flour and fold them into the egg mixture. Pour into the sweet pastry shells and bake in the oven for 10 minutes until the filling is lightly set and has formed a thin crust over the surface.

Remove the tartlets from the oven and lower the temperature to 325°F (160°C). Arrange a ring of walnut halves around the outside edge of each tart and return them to the oven; bake for another 10 minutes until completely set.

Meanwhile, for the athol brose cream, whisk the cream until it begins to thicken. Slowly whisk in the honey and then the whisky until the mixture forms soft peaks.

Remove the tartlets from the oven and leave them to cool a little until warm. Then carefully lift them out of the pans onto dessert plates and serve with some of the athol brose cream.

DRAMBUIE AND PRUNE CUSTARD TART

Most people associate prunes with Armagnac, probably because they come from the same area of southwest France. However, they also conjoin sublimely with Drambuie, especially the Agen prunes, which are plump, sweet, and flavorsome. Drambuie is not only my favorite post-prandial tipple, but the liqueur that I use most often in my cooking. There's just something in that combination of honey, spices, and whisky that brings out or accentuates other flavors. The whisky with the history and the mystery! Mine's a large one, thank you!

Serves 8

12 oz (350 g) dried Agen or other
   good-quality prunes
5 tablespoons Drambuie
1 tablespoon soft light brown sugar
1¼ cups heavy cream
⅔ cup milk

4 medium farm-fresh eggs
¼ cup superfine sugar
1 teaspoon vanilla extract
1 tablespoon all-purpose flour
1 (10 inch) (25 cm) Sweet Pastry tart shell
  (see page 188)
confectioners' sugar, to decorate
pouring cream (optional), to serve

Make a slit in the side of each prune and hook out the pits with the tip of a knife. Reshape the fruit and put them into a bowl with the Drambuie and brown sugar. Cover and leave to soak overnight. The next day, slide a baking sheet into the oven and preheat it to 350°F (180°C).

Drain the prunes, reserving any juices. Put the cream and milk into a pan and slowly bring just up to a boil. Meanwhile, whisk the eggs, sugar, vanilla, and flour until well combined. Whisk in the hot cream and milk and any Drambuie juices left over from the prunes.

Arrange the prunes over the bottom of the pastry shell. Pull out the oven shelf with the baking sheet and slide on the tart pan; then pour over the custard mixture. Carefully slide the shelf back into the oven and bake the tart for 30–35 minutes until just set. Remove from the oven and leave to cool. Sprinkle the edges of the tart with a little confectioners' sugar and serve cut into wedges, with a little extra pouring cream if you like.

LITTLE SCOTTISH BUTTERSCOTCH POTS
with Viennese shortbread fingers

These little puds are like a cross between a crème brûlée (without the top) and a mousse. What makes them so special is the "toffee," which you make by boiling a can of sweetened condensed milk until it caramelizes inside the can. All they then need is a thin layer of unwhipped cream flooded over the top. If you like, you can use the shortbread fingers to scoop out the mixture. Yum!

Serves 6

1 (7 oz) (200 g) can sweetened
    condensed milk
6 medium farm-fresh egg yolks
generous 1½ cups heavy cream, plus extra
    to serve

For the Viennese shortbread fingers
    (makes 12):

5 tablespoons butter, slightly softened
3 tablespoons confectioners' sugar, plus extra
    for dusting
3 tablespoons cornstarch
¼ cup all-purpose flour

Place the unopened can of condensed milk in a pan and cover it with cold water. Bring to a boil and leave to simmer for 3 hours, topping up the water every now and then so that it always covers the can. Leave to cool in the water.

Preheat the oven to 300°F (150°C). Open the can of "toffee" and scrape it into a bowl. Stir in the egg yolks and then gradually stir in the cream until you have a smooth mixture. Strain it into a pitcher and then pour it evenly into six 3 inch (7.5 cm) ramekins. Place them in a small roasting pan and pour in boiling water until it comes halfway up the sides of the dishes. Slide the roasting pann onto the middle shelf of the oven and cook for 20–25 minutes until just set but still a little wobbly. Remove the ramekins from the roasting pan, leave to cool and then cover and chill for at least a couple of hours.

For the shortbread fingers, increase the oven temperature to 350°F (180°C). Lightly grease and flour a baking sheet. Beat the butter with the sugar until pale and creamy. Sift the cornstarch and flour together, then beat into the butter mixture until smooth. Spoon the mixture into a piping bag fitted with a large star tip and pipe twelve 3 inch (7.5 cm) fingers spaced well apart onto the prepared baking sheet. Chill in the refrigerator for 30 minutes. Bake the fingers for 10–12 minutes until golden. Leave to go cold and then carefully lift them off the baking sheet.

To serve, pour a thin layer of unwhipped cream onto the top of each butterscotch pot. Dust the shortbread fingers with a little confectioners' sugar and serve alongside the pots.

AMARETTI AND PEACH TRIFLE

with mascarpone cream

There are a lot of trifle variations doing the rounds in Britain at the moment and this Italian-inspired version is my effort. Use top-quality white peaches if you can, but there are some pretty good canned ones around, although they are generally more expensive than the fresh ones. I like to serve a glass of chilled Italian dessert wine with this trifle. Please note, in case it's a problem for you, that this recipe has raw eggs in it.

Serves 6

5 oz (150 g) amaretti cookies

3 tablespoons Kirsch or amontillado sherry

6 large, juicy fresh peaches

10 oz (275 g) mascarpone

2 medium farm-fresh eggs, separated

¼ cup superfine sugar

⅔ cup whipping cream

5 tablespoons granulated sugar

Place the amaretti cookies in a deep, glass serving dish and sprinkle over the Kirsch or sherry. Set aside, turning the cookies over every now and then, until they have soaked up all the liquid. Meanwhile, place the peaches in a large bowl and cover with boiling water. Leave for 30 seconds, then drain and cover with cold water. Peel off the skins; halve to remove the pits and then cut the peaches into slices directly over the trifle bowl so that you don't lose any of the juices. Spread the fruit out into an even layer.

Beat the mascarpone and egg yolks together in a bowl until smooth and creamy. Beat in the sugar. Whisk the cream until it just begins to thicken and then gently stir it into the mascarpone. Whisk the egg whites into soft peaks and lightly fold them into the mascarpone cream. The finished mixture should be quite soft and light. Spoon the mixture over the top of the peaches. Lightly level the top and chill in the refrigerator for 3–4 hours.

Now put the granulated sugar into a heavy-bottomed pan and cook over a medium–high heat until it has melted and turned into liquid caramel. Meanwhile, mark a round about 1 inch (2.5 cm) smaller than the diameter of your trifle dish on a piece of nonstick baking parchment. Remove the caramel from the heat and drizzle it back and forth over the paper using a spoon, taking care not to go outside the edge of the round. What you want to do is create a sort of caramel cobweb. Leave it to cool and go hard; then carefully lift it off the paper and lower it on top of the trifle just before serving.

CHAMPAGNE JELLIES

with a citrus fruit salad

These lovely translucent jellies look stunning with the multicolored citrus pieces floating in their passion fruit sea. I'm getting a bit carried away with the prose, but this is a refreshing and stylish way to end a meal.

Serves 4

1½ cups champagne or sparkling dry
   white wine

1¼ cups superfine sugar

1 (¼ oz) (10 g) envelope unflavored gelatin or
   4 × 3 g sheets leaf of gelatin

For the citrus fruit salad:

12 passion fruit

superfine sugar, to taste

2 ruby grapefruit

2 oranges

1 lemon

1 lime

For the jellies, put the champagne or sparkling wine and sugar into a pan and leave over a gentle heat until the sugar has dissolved. Meanwhile, if using leaf gelatin, leave it to soak in cold water for a few minutes; then lift it out, stir it into the champagne mixture, and leave until dissolved. If using powdered gelatin, put 3 tablespoons of cold water into a small pan, sprinkle over the powder, and leave it to "sponge" for 5 minutes. Heat very gently until clear and then stir into the champagne mixture. Pour into 4 wet dariole or mini-dessert molds and leave to set in the refrigerator overnight.

The next day, make the citrus fruit salad. Halve the passion fruit and scoop out the pulp into a sieve. Set over a small pan. Press out the juice with a wooden spoon and reserve a few of the seeds for decoration. Discard the rest. Cook the juice over a gentle heat until it thickens, then stir in a little superfine sugar to taste. Leave to go cold and chill until needed.

Slice the top and bottom off each citrus fruit and then cut away all the skin and white pith with a small, sharp knife. Cut either side of each dividing membrane to remove the fruit in neat segments and then stir them into the passion fruit juice.

To serve, dip the molds very briefly in warm water and turn the jellies out into the centers of 4 dessert plates. Spoon the citrus fruit salad around them and sprinkle with the reserved passion fruit seeds.

Crème Brûlées

I'm pretty sure I'm on record as having stated that vanilla is the only flavoring that should be used in crème brûlée. However, a period of experimentation has caused me to change my mind on that one, and I offer you four alternatives. The secret of making brûlées that set in the refrigerator is (1) to whisk the egg yolks over simmering water until a strand from the whisk will lie on the surface of the mixture, and (2) to ensure that the cream is just about to boil over before pouring it onto the yolks. That way the mix cooks out in seconds rather than the more usual quarter of an hour of stirring. Always use a wooden spoon to stir the mix once it is back in the pan and use a side-to-side motion rather than a circular one. This moves the milk about more and prevents that scrambled egg thing happening in the bottom of the pan.

EGG NOG CRÈME BRÛLÉE

Here, Advocaat brings out the egginess in the brûlée mixture, but it still needs the vanilla to make it sing.

Serves 6

2½ cups heavy cream
6 medium farm-fresh egg yolks
¼ cup superfine sugar

For the flavoring and topping:

1 vanilla bean
6 tablespoons Advocaat liqueur
½ teaspoon freshly grated nutmeg
6 heaped teaspoons Demerara sugar

Split open the vanilla bean and scrape out the seeds into a pan. Add the cream and the bean and slowly bring up to a boil. Put the egg yolks and superfine sugar into a bowl and rest over a pan on simmering water. Whisk until the mixture is very pale and thick.

Just before the cream boils over the sides of the pan, pour two-thirds onto the egg yolks and whisk together. Pour the mixture back into the pan containing the remaining cream and stir over a low heat for 2–3 minutes until it is thick and coats the back of a spoon. Remove the pan from the heat and stir for another couple of minutes. Remove the vanilla bean and stir in the Advocaat and the nutmeg. Pour the mixture into six 3 inch (7.5 cm) ramekins, taking the mixture right to the top. Leave them to set in the refrigerator for at least 6 hours and preferably overnight.

To serve, preheat the broiler to its highest setting (or you can use a blowtorch). Sprinkle the tops of the brûlées with the Demerara sugar, making sure you take it right to the edges of the ramekins, and slide them under the broiler for 2–3 minutes until the sugar has caramelized. Remove and leave until the sugar toppings have cooled and gone hard before serving.

ESPRESSO COFFEE BRÛLÉE

You need top-quality coffee beans for the right flavor here. Espresso has that lovely, slightly bitter edge. Otherwise, cheat and use 2 teaspoons instant espresso coffee granules.

Serves 6

2½ cups heavy cream
6 medium farm-fresh egg yolks
¼ cup superfine sugar

For the flavouring and topping:

1½ tablespoons ground espresso coffee beans
3 tablespoons coffee liqueur, such as
    Tía Maria
6 heaped teaspoons soft light brown sugar

Put the ground coffee and the cream into a pan and slowly bring up to a boil. Put the egg yolks and superfine sugar into a bowl and rest over a pan of simmering water. Whisk until the mixture is very pale and thick.

Just before the cream boils over the sides of the pan, pour two-thirds onto the egg yolks through a muslin-lined sieve and whisk together. Pour the mixture back into the pan containing the remaining cream and stir over a low heat for 2–3 minutes until it is thick and coats the back of a spoon. Remove the pan from the heat and stir for another couple of minutes. Stir in the coffee liqueur and pour the mixture into six 3 inch (7.5 cm) ramekins, taking the mixture right to the top. Leave them to set in the refrigerator for at least 6 hours and preferably overnight.

To serve, preheat the broiler to its highest setting (or you can use a blowtorch). Sprinkle the top of the brûlées with the soft brown sugar, making sure you take it right to the edges of the ramekins, and slide them under the broiler for 2–3 minutes until the sugar has caramelized. Remove and leave until the sugar topping has cooled and gone hard before serving.

ORANGE CRÈME BRÛLÉE

Drambuie again, this time with one of its favorite partners, oranges. Use small, sweet, seedless oranges for this.

Serves 6

2–3 small, thin-skinned oranges
6 tablespoons Drambuie liqueur
finely grated zest (or pared zest) of
½ small orange

2–4 whole cloves
2½ cups heavy cream
6 medium farm-fresh egg yolks
¼ cup superfine sugar, plus 6 heaped
teaspoons for sprinkling

Slice the top and the bottom off each orange and sit each one on a board. Slice away the outer skin so that there is no white pith left behind and then slice each orange across into thin slices. Place about 3 slices in the bottom of each 3 inch (7.5 cm) ramekin and spoon over 1 tablespoon of the Drambuie.

Put the orange zest, the cloves, and the cream into a pan and slowly bring up to a boil. Put the egg yolks and sugar into a bowl and rest over a pan on simmering water. Whisk until the mixture is very pale and thick.

Just before the cream boils over the sides of the pan, pour two-thirds onto the egg yolks and whisk together. Pour the mixture back into the pan containing the remaining cream and stir over a low heat for 2–3 minutes until it is thick and coats the back of a spoon. Remove the pan from the heat and stir for another couple of minutes. Pour the mixture through a muslin-lined sieve into the ramekins, taking the mixture right to the top. Leave them to set in the refrigerator for at least 6 hours and preferably overnight.

To serve, preheat the broiler to its highest setting (or you can use a blowtorch). Sprinkle the top of the brûlées with the sugar, making sure you take it right to the edges of the ramekins, and slide them under the broiler for 2–3 minutes until the sugar has caramelized. Remove and leave until the sugar topping has cooled and gone hard before serving.

SUMMER BERRY BRÛLÉE

The great thing about this is the lovely puddle of fruity caramel juices at the bottom of the pot, which soak into the custard.

Serves 6

5 tablespoons granulated sugar, plus 6 heaped teaspoons

6 oz (175 g) mixed prepared blueberries, black currants, and red currants

6 oz (175 g) raspberries and halved small strawberries

1 vanilla bean

2½ cups heavy cream

6 medium farm-fresh egg yolks

¼ cup superfine caster sugar

Put the 5 tablespoons of granulated sugar into a heavy-bottomed pan and cook over a medium heat until it dissolves and cooks to a light brown caramel. Take the pan off the heat and stir in the blueberries, black currants, and red currants. The heat of the caramel will cook these fruits a little but the caramel will start to harden around them so return it to a low heat and warm it gently until it has dissolved. Stir in the raspberries and strawberries and divide the mixture between six 3 inch (7.5 cm) ramekins.

Split open the vanilla bean and scrape out the seeds into a pan. Add the cream and the bean and slowly bring up to a boil. Put the egg yolks and superfine sugar into a bowl and rest over a pan on simmering water. Whisk until the mixture is very pale and thick.

Just before the cream boils over the sides of the pan, pour two-thirds onto the egg yolks and whisk together. Pour the mixture back into the pan containing the remaining cream and stir over a low heat for 2–3 minutes until it is thick and coats the back of a spoon. Remove the pan from the heat and stir for another couple of minutes. Remove the vanilla bean and pour the mixture into the ramekins, taking the mixture right to the top. Leave them to set in the refrigerator for at least 6 hours and preferably overnight.

To serve, preheat the broiler to its highest setting (or you can use a blowtorch). Sprinkle the top of the brûlées with the remaining granulated sugar, making sure you take it right to the edges of the ramekins, and slide them under the broiler for 2–3 minutes until the sugar has caramelized. Remove and leave until the sugar topping has cooled and gone hard before serving.

BLOOD ORANGE TRICKLE TART

with a compote of oranges and caramel chip ice cream

Blood oranges are worth finding when they are in season as they not only have a fabulous color, but also a more intense flavor than their more ordinary relatives. The crunchy caramel ice-cream gives the killer blow here. Warm tart streaked with syrup, orange salad, and crunchy caramel ice cream. Who could ask for more!

Serves 8-12

½ cup butter, softened

¾ cup superfine sugar

finely grated zest of 1 large orange

2 medium farm-fresh eggs

1⅓ cups self-rising flour

5 tablespoons freshly squeezed blood
   orange juice

1 (10 inch) (25 cm) Sweet Pastry pie shell
   (see page 188)

½ cup granulated sugar

For the caramel chip ice cream:

1 vanilla bean

2½ cups milk

6 medium farm-fresh egg yolks

5 tablespoons superfiner sugar

1¼ cups heavy cream

½ cup granulated sugar

For the compote of oranges:

3 blood oranges

3 small, thin-skinned ordinary oranges

2 tablespoons superfine sugar or to taste

First make the ice cream so that it has plenty of time to freeze. Split open the vanilla bean and scrape out the seeds into a pan. Add the milk and the vanilla bean and bring to the boil. Set aside for 20 minutes to let the vanilla flavor the milk. Then bring the milk back to a boil. Meanwhile, beat the egg yolks and sugar together in a bowl until pale and creamy. Remove the vanilla bean from the milk and whisk the hot milk into the egg yolks. Return the mixture to the pan and cook over a gentle heat, stirring continuously, until the mixture lightly coats the back of a wooden spoon. Pour into a bowl and leave to cool. Stir in the heavy cream and leave it to chill in the refrigerator for 1 hour. Now you can either churn the mixture in an ice cream maker or pour it into a shallow plastic box and leave it in the freezer until almost firm. If you do the latter, scrape the mixture into a food processor and whizz it until smooth – this will break down all the ice crystals in the mixture. Scrape the mixture back into the box, return to the freezer, and leave once more until almost firm.

While the ice cream is either churning in the machine or just before you are ready to whizz the handmade ice cream for the last time, put the granulated sugar into a heavy-bottomed pan and leave over a medium–high heat until it dissolves and cooks to a golden brown caramel. Pour onto a nonstick baking sheet and leave to cool and go hard. Whizz the ice cream for the last time. Break the caramel into little pieces and stir them into the ice cream. Return the ice cream to the freezer until very firm or until required. If you make your ice cream some time in advance, remove from the freezer to the refrigerator about 30 minutes before you want to serve it to let it soften slightly.

For the tart, preheat the oven to 350°F (180°C). To make the filling, cream the butter, sugar, and orange zest together in a bowl until very pale and thick. Beat the eggs into the creamed mixture one at a time, adding a spoonful of the flour with the second egg. Sift over the rest of the flour and gently fold in with 1 tablespoon of the orange juice to give the mixture a dropping consistency. Spread it into the bottom of the sweet pastry shell and bake in the oven for 30 minutes until golden brown.

Meanwhile, strain the rest of the blood orange juice into a bowl and stir in the granulated sugar. Also prepare the compote of oranges. Slice the tops and bottoms off the oranges and then cut away all the skin and white pith with a small, sharp knife. Cut either side of each dividing membrane to remove the fruit in neat segments and mix them together in a bowl with the sugar. As soon as the tart is ready, remove it from the oven and quickly spoon over the blood orange syrup mixture, leaving some of the sponge filling untouched. This will give the tart an almost stripy look when you cut into it. Leave it for a few minutes to cool slightly and let the syrup soak into the sponge.

Remove the tart from the pan and cut it into wedges. Place one piece on each plate and spoon some of the orange compote alongside. Add a scoop of the caramel chip ice cream and serve the tart while it is still warm.

WARM BUTTER CAKE

with plums poached in kir

This butter cake is very rich and very moreish. It can be cooked a couple of days ahead and kept in an airtight container if you wish. The plums improve with keeping, making this an easy dessert for a dinner party. Just warm the cake in a low oven for 10 minutes and heat the plums gently in a saucepan, but don't let them boil. Be warned, there will be requests for second helpings.

Serves 8

6 medium farm-fresh egg yolks
generous 2 cups all-purpose flour
generous ¾ cup superfine sugar
1 cup butter, at room temperature and cut into
    small pieces, plus extra for greasing

For the plums:

2 lb (900 g) (about 24) red-skinned or
    Victoria plums
¾ cups superfine sugar
1¼ cups white wine
2 tablespoons crème de cassis liqueur (kir)

Preheat the oven to 375°F (190°C). Grease a 1½ inch (4 cm) deep, 10 inch (25 cm) flan or pie pan with plenty of butter. Lightly beat the egg yolks together in a small bowl. Sift the flour into a bowl and make a dip in the middle. Add almost all the egg yolks (leaving about 1 tablespoon for glazing the tart at the end), the sugar, and the butter, and gradually mix the ingredients together until you have a smooth dough. Transfer the dough to the prepared pan and press it out evenly using lightly floured hands, making sure that the top is smooth. Brush the cake with the reserved egg yolk and then mark with a squiggly criss-cross pattern using the back of a fork. Bake the cake for 15 minutes; then lower the oven temperature to 325°F (160°C) and bake for another 15 minutes until the top is golden.

While the cake is baking, halve the plums and remove the pits. Put the sugar and wine into a large pan and bring to a boil. Add the crème de cassis and the prepared plums and leave to simmer very gently for 1–2 minutes until just tender (this will depend on the ripeness of your plums). Lift the plums out of the syrup with a slotted spoon and transfer to a shallow dish. Boil the remaining syrup for 5–6 minutes until it has reduced to a coating consistency. Leave it to cool a little and then pour it back over the plums. This is quite important because if the syrup is too hot, it will continue to cook the plums even more, which you don't want. They must be served warm, too, not hot.

Remove the butter cake from the oven and leave it to cool in the pan for 15 minutes; then turn it out onto a wire rack. Serve the cake warm, cut into wedges, with the poached plums.

STEM GINGER AND MOLASSES PUDDINGS
with ginger toffee sauce

A type of sponge that doesn't have to be steamed, these puddings have a lovely dense, moist texture with the flavor of ginger permeating every mouthful.

Serves 4

6 oz (175 g) preserved ginger in syrup

2 tablespoons ginger syrup

⅔ cup all-purpose flour

¼ teaspoon ground ginger

¼ teaspoon baking powder

¼ rounded teaspoon baking soda

1 medium farm-fresh egg

3 tablespoons butter, softened

⅓ cup dark brown sugar

1 tablespoon molasses

For the ginger toffee sauce:

⅓ cup dark brown sugar

¼ cup butter

⅔ cup heavy cream

Slide a baking sheet onto the middle shelf of the oven and preheat it to 350°F (180°C). Lightly grease four ½ cup nonstick dessert molds with a little butter.

Put the ginger and the syrup into a food processor and give it a whizz until the ginger is finely chopped but not completely smooth. Spoon half of it into a small pan and add the sauce ingredients to it. Set aside.

Sift the flour, ground ginger, baking powder, and baking soda into a bowl. Add the egg, softened butter, sugar, and molasses, and beat together until smooth. Beat in 5 tablespoons (3 fl oz) of warm water and the remaining whizzed ginger.

Spoon the mixture into the prepared molds and bake in the oven for 20–25 minutes. Meanwhile, stir the sauce ingredients together over a low heat until heated through and smooth. Turn out the puddings onto dessert plates and spoon over the ginger toffee sauce. Serve immediately.

CROWDIE

with muscat-soaked raisins and oatmeal cookies

A dessert for those odd people who don't have a sweet tooth. It's based loosely on a classic French dessert called coeur à la crème, made with a curd-like cheese. I prefer it made with crowdie, which is Scottish cheese curds; ricotta is a great alternative. Some supermarkets sell really big, fat, jumbo raisins and these are best for this recipe.

Serves 6

¼ cup Muscat Beaumes de Venise or sweet
    dessert wine, plus 1 tablespoon
1 tablespoon superfine sugar
Scant 1 cup muscatel raisins
1 lb (450 g) crowdie or ricotta cheese

For the oatmeal cookies:
1 cup whole wheat flour
½ cup medium oatmeal
2 teaspoons soft light brown sugar
rounded ¼ teaspoon baking powder
a pinch of Maldon or sea salt
5 tablespoons butter
1 tablespoon milk

Warm the ¼ cup Muscat Beaumes de Venise and the sugar together in a small pan. Pour this over the raisins, cover and leave to soak overnight. Also, line six 3 inch (7.5 cm) metal pastry rings with small squares of damp muslin and set them on a fine-meshed cooling rack. Spoon in the cheese and level the surface; then cover with the overhanging muslin. Rest the rack over a baking sheet and slide it into the refrigerator. Leave the cheeses to drain overnight.

For the cookies, preheat the oven to 350°F (180°C). Mix the flour, oatmeal, sugar, baking powder, and salt together in a bowl. Rub in the butter until the mixture looks like fine breadcrumbs. Stir in the milk to make a soft dough and knead very gently into a ball. On a work surface lightly dusted with flour, roll out the dough to a thickness of about ¼ inch (3 mm). Cut into 2 inch (5 cm) cookies, rekneading and rolling the trimmings until you have about 24 cookies. Place on a lightly greased baking sheet and prick a couple of times with a fork. Bake for 10–12 minutes until crisp and golden, then remove from the oven and leave to cool for 5 minutes. Transfer to a cooling rack and leave to go cold. Keep in an airtight tin if you make these the day before you need them.

Unmold the fresh cheeses into the centers of 6 small plates. Stir the 1 tablespoon of Muscat Beaumes de Venise into the raisins, then spoon some on top of and around the cheeses. Serve each cheese with about 4 of the oatmeal cookies.

LIME AND PISTACHIO KULFI

with tropical fruits in a ginger and lemon grass syrup

Kulfi is an Indian ice cream made with milk instead of cream. A large quantity of milk is slowly reduced in a large pan until you end up with real evaporated milk, which gives this finished dessert a lovely, rich flavor. I like to shape these in dariole molds, but rinsed yogurt containers work brilliantly too. The fruit salad adds a nice sharp contrast to the ice creams.

Serves 6

8½ cups whole milk
½ cup shelled pistachio nuts
3 tablespoons superfine sugar
½ teaspoon rosewater
1½ tablespoons ground almonds
⅔ cup light cream
zest of 2 limes, finely grated

For the tropical fruit salad:

½ cup cold water
¼ cup granulated sugar
½ stalk of lemon grass
zest of ½ lemon, grated
zest of 1 lime, grated
3 slices fresh ginger root
1 small sprig of fresh mint, plus very small
    leaves to decorate
8 oz (225 g) tropical fruits, such as mango,
    pawpaw, pineapple, kiwi fruit and bananas
2 tablespoons lime juice

Bring the milk to a boil in as large a pan as you have and leave it to simmer vigorously, stirring regularly to get rid of the skin as it forms and to make sure that it doesn't catch on the bottom of the pan. Do this for 1 hour or until it has reduced by two-thirds to about 5¼ cups. Meanwhile, preheat the oven to 400°F (200°C). Spread the pistachio nuts out on a baking sheet and roast in the oven for 5 minutes until crisp. Leave to cool and then chop finely. Sprinkle some of the nuts in a thin layer on the base of 6 dariole molds, small yogurt containers, or 3 inch (7.5 cm) ramekins.

Strain the reduced milk into a clean pan and stir in the sugar, rosewater, and almonds. Simmer for 2–3 minutes more. Remove the pan from the heat and stir in the cream, the rest of the pistachio nuts, and the lime zest. Leave the mixture to cool and then chill it in the refrigerator for 1 hour until really cold. Now churn the mixture in an ice cream machine, or pour it into a shallow plastic box and put it into the freezer, beating the mixture every now and then as it freezes to break up the ice crystals. When it is almost firm, spoon the mixture into the prepared molds, cover with plastic wrap and freeze until firm.

For the fruit salad, put the water and sugar into a small pan and leave over a low heat until the sugar has completely dissolved. Cut the lemon grass in half lengthwise and bruise it lightly with the end of a rolling pin. Add half the lemon and lime zest, the lemon grass, and ginger to the syrup and bring it up to a boil. Leave it to simmer for 5 minutes; then take it off the heat, add the sprig of mint, and leave to cool. Strain the syrup into a bowl and chill in the refrigerator until really cold. Meanwhile, cut the rest of the lemon and lime zest into fine needle-shreds. Drop them into boiling water, leave for a few seconds, and then drain and refresh under cold water. Set aside.

Just before serving, peel the fruits and cut them into small, neat pieces. Stir them into the chilled syrup with the lemon and lime shreds and the lime juice. Unmold the kulfi into the centers of 6 dessert plates and spoon around some of the tropical fruits and the syrup. Scatter the small mint leaves over the fruits and serve straightaway.

DRAMBUIE ORANGES

This is one of my all-time favorite desserts and without a doubt one of the easiest – you can even make it in advance. Sometimes simple food is the best.

Serves 4

6–8 small, juicy, thin-skinned oranges
4 tablespoons Drambuie

Slice the top and the bottom off each orange and sit each one on a board. Cut away the outer skin so that there is no white pith left behind, and then slice each orange across into thin slices. Arrange the slices overlapping in the centers of 4 large dessert plates, drizzle over the Drambuie and serve straightaway. Alternatively, place the orange slices in a shallow dish with the Drambuie, cover and leave to chill in the refrigerator for 3–4 hours, during which time the juice from the oranges will develop a wonderful-tasting sauce with the Drambuie. Arrange on serving plates as before and serve while the slices are still chilled.

CRÈME FRAÎCHE TERRINE

with Calvados cream sauce and cidered pears

A big slice of vanilla-flavored mousse with caramelized pears and a Calvados and caramel cream sauce – need I say more? All right – use ripe comice pears and don't eat too much in one sitting.

Serves 8-12

5 teaspoons unflavored gelatin

2 cups natural yogurt (whole-milk or Greek)

scant 1 cup crème fraîche

5 tablespoons superfine sugar

⅔ cup whipping cream

2 teaspoons vanilla extract

2 medium farm-fresh egg whites

For the Calvados cream sauce:

½ cup superfine sugar

1¼ cups heavy cream

3 tablespoons Calvados, Pommeau or brandy

For the cidered pears:

4–6 pears

3 tablespoons unsalted butter

3 tablespoons sugar

3 tablespoons dry cider

Put 5 tablespoons of cold water into a small pan. Sprinkle over the gelatin and leave it to "sponge" for 5 minutes.

Mix the yogurt, crème fraîche, and sugar together in a large bowl until smooth. Lightly whip the cream until it begins to thicken and fold it into the yogurt mixture with the vanilla extract. Place the pan of gelatin over a low heat and leave until clear. Stir it into the creamy mixture, making sure it is mixed in well. Whisk the egg whites in a separate bowl until they form soft peaks – the tips of the peaks should flop over, not stand upright. Fold 1 large spoonful into the yogurt mixture to loosen it slightly, then gently fold in the remainder. Pour the mixture into a 3 inch (7.5 cm) deep, 3 × 10 inch (7.5 × 25 cm) terrine dish (a Le Creuset terrine is ideal). Cover with plastic wrap and chill in the refrigerator for at least 6 hours or preferably overnight.

For the Calvados cream sauce, put the sugar and 2 tablespoons of water into a pan and stir over a high heat until the sugar has dissolved. Now leave it to cook without stirring until it has turned a rich amber color. Take the pan off the heat, pour in the cream, and stir until all the caramel has dissolved into it – you might need to return it to a very low heat for a minute or two. Remove from the heat, leave to cool, and then stir in the Calvados.

Just before you are ready to serve, cook the cidered pears. Cut the pears into quarters and remove the cores; then peel. Cut each piece in half once more. Melt the butter in a large, heavy-bottomed skillet and, as soon as it starts to foam, add the pears and fry over a high heat for 1 minute on each side until golden brown. Sprinkle over the sugar and the cider, and continue to cook for no more than 2 minutes until the cider has reduced and formed a sugary syrup with the butter and sugar.

To serve, dip the terrine briefly into warm water. Invert it onto a serving plate or board and cut it into slices. Place one piece on each plate and arrange a few pieces of the cidered pears alongside. Pour the Calvados cream sauce over the terrine and the pears and serve immediately.

BROWN SUGAR MERINGUES

with lime cream and mangoes

It's important to use good-quality brown sugar here, and not that stuff which is just refined white sugar with a coating of molasses. Make sure you sieve it so that there are no lumps before you add it to the egg whites. When I was wee, meringues were a huge treat and I still insist on serving these up in the restaurant in big paper cases. It reminds me of a time when the thought of a meringue after tea would occupy my thoughts all day.

Serves 6

3 medium farm-fresh egg whites
1 cup light brown sugar, sieved, plus a little
    extra for sprinkling
3 small ripe but firm mangoes
6 fresh mint sprigs, to decorate

For the lime cream:
1 ¼ cups whipping cream
finely grated zest of 2 limes
3 tablespoons lime juice (about 1 ½ limes)
1 tablespoon superfine sugar

Preheat the oven to 225°F (110°C). Line a large baking sheet with nonstick baking parchment. Whisk the egg whites in a large, very clean bowl until they form stiff peaks. Very gradually whisk in the sugar, a spoonful at a time, making sure that you whisk the mixture well between each addition to ensure that the sugar has dissolved and combined with the egg whites. This is important in order to prevent the meringues from losing all their volume as muscovado sugar is quite moist and heavy.

Spoon the mixture into 6 meringues on the baking sheet and sprinkle the tops with a little more sugar. Bake for a minimum of 4 hours until very dry and hard. Cool and set aside.

To serve, peel the mangoes and then slice the flesh away from either side of the thin, flat pit in the center. Cut each piece lengthwise into long, thin slices. Whip the cream with the lime zest, lime juice, and sugar until it forms soft peaks. Spoon a little of the cream into the centers of 6 dessert plates. Arrange slices of mango on top like the points of a star and then spoon on the rest of the cream. Place a meringue in the center of each star and decorate with a sprig of mint.

HAZELNUT PAVLOVA CAKE

with raspberry cream

Ground nuts give a firmer texture and good, nutty flavor when added to the mix of a basic pavlova. Layered up with raspberries and whipped cream and dusted with confectioners' sugar, it looks the part. It does need the fruit syrup to provide extra juice and zing, though. If you like, you could use pistachios instead of hazelnuts – these will give a lush green tinge to the finished meringue.

Serves 12

1⅓ cups shelled hazelnuts

1¼ cups egg whites (from about
  8–10 farm-fresh medium eggs)

2 cups superfine sugar

2 tablespoons balsamic vinegar

2 heaped teaspoons cornstarch

2 cups whipping cream

3 tablespoons eau de framboises, eau de vie
  or Kirsch

3 tablespoons confectioners' sugar, plus extra
  for dusting

12 oz (350 g) fresh raspberries

For the red fruit syrup:

½ cup Stock Syrup (see page 188)

8 oz (225 g) mixed summer fruits, such as
  strawberries, raspberries, blackberries,
  red currants, and black currants, prepared
  as necessary

Preheat the oven to 350°F (180°C). Grease and line the bottom of two 12 inch (30 cm) spring form cake pans with baking parchment. Spread the hazelnuts on a baking sheet and roast them in the oven for 10 minutes or so until they are richly golden. Leave to cool; then tip them into a clean dish towel and rub off the skins. Transfer the nuts to a food processor and give them a quick blitz for a few seconds until they are completely ground. Lower the oven temperature to 325°F (160°C).

Place the egg whites in a large bowl or a food mixer and whisk them until they form soft peaks. Continue to whisk, adding the sugar a spoonful at a time. Make sure you mix the sugar thoroughly into the egg whites before you add the next spoonful. When all the sugar has been added, mix the balsamic vinegar with the cornstarch and whisk this into the whites for 6–8 minutes until the meringue is very thick and shiny.

Fold the finely chopped hazelnuts into the meringue mixture. Divide it evenly between the prepared pans and spread it out level with the back of a spoon. The mixture should be no more than ¾ inch (2 cm) thick. Bake the pavlovas in the preheated oven for 30 minutes until they have risen up and are lightly browned on top. Remove them from the oven and leave to cool for about 2 hours before removing them from their pans.

For the red fruit syrup, bring the stock syrup up to a simmer in a small pan. Add the summer fruits and cook gently for 15–20 minutes. Transfer the mixture to a blender and process until smooth. Press the mixture through a fine sieve into a bowl and leave to cool. Then cover and chill until needed.

To assemble the pavlova, whip the cream with the eau de framboises, eau de vie, or Kirsch and confectioners' sugar into soft peaks. Gently fold in the raspberries so that they break up very slightly and the cream thickens a little more. Sandwich the two meringues together with the cream. Transfer to a plate and leave in the refrigerator for 4 hours to firm up.

To serve, dust the top of the pavlova with confectioners' sugar and cut it into 12 wedges. Lift them onto serving plates and serve with the red fruit syrup drizzled around the edges of the plates.

BUTTERSCOTCH TART

What could be more Scottish than butterscotch? The rich, smooth texture of the butterscotch-flavored filling goes beautifully with my almost shortbread-like pastry so that all it needs is a just a little more cream to serve.

Serves 8

¼ cup butter
½ cup soft light brown sugar
¼ cup granulated sugar
½ cup light corn syrup

1¼ cups heavy cream, plus extra for serving (optional)
1 teaspoon vanilla extract
4 medium farm-fresh eggs
1 (10 inch) (25 cm) Sweet Pastry tart shell (see page 188)

Preheat the oven to 300°F (150°C). For the filling, put the butter, soft brown sugar, granulated sugar, and light corn syrup into a medium-size pan. Stir over a low heat until the sugars have dissolved and then cook gently for 5 minutes until smooth and thick. Remove the pan from the heat and stir in the heavy cream and the vanilla extract. Leave to cool for 10 minutes and then beat in the eggs. Strain the mixture into the pastry shell and bake for 35–40 minutes until just set. Remove the tart from the oven and leave to cool for about 30 minutes. Cut it into wedges and serve with a little lightly whipped cream if you wish.

DRAMBUIE CREAMS

with a raspberry and orange compote

Drambuie and oranges again – I can't get enough – but this time the Drambuie is used to flavor panna-cotta-like creams and served with a fresh-tasting combination of raspberries and orange juice.

Serves 6

1¼ cups heavy cream

1 cup milk

¼ cup superfine sugar

2 teaspoons unflavored gelatin or
   2½ x 3 g sheets leaf gelatin

4 tablespoons Drambuie liqueur

For the raspberry and orange compote:

1 lb (450 g) fresh raspberries

¼ cup superfine sugar

finely grated zest of ½ orange

¼ cup freshly squeezed orange juice

For the Drambuie creams, soak the leaf gelatin, if using, in cold water for a few minutes. Put the cream, milk, sugar, and leaf gelatin into a pan and leave over a low heat until the sugar and gelatin have dissolved. If using powdered gelatin, put 2 tablespoons of cold water into a small pan. Sprinkle over the gelatin and leave to "sponge" for 5 minutes. Place the pan over a low heat and leave until the gelatin is clear. Stir into the cream and milk mixture, followed by the Drambuie. Pour the mixture into 6 dariole molds or 7.5 cm (3 inch) ramekins, cover and chill for 4 hours or until set.

For the raspberry and orange compote, put 8 oz (225 g) of the raspberries into a bowl with the sugar and the orange zest, and crush with the back of a fork into a smooth purée. Press the mixture through a fine sieve into a bowl to remove all the seeds. Stir in the orange juice and chill in the refrigerator for 1 hour or until needed.

To serve, dip the dariole molds or ramekins very briefly into warm water. Unmold the creams into the center or slightly to one side of each dessert plate. Stir the rest of the raspberries into the raspberry and orange sauce and spoon some around the creams.

FREE-FORMED APPLE TARTS

with mincemeat ice cream

Free-form apple tarts have an organic, rustic appearance which appeals to me and it means you don't need any special pans. These tarts are dead easy to make.

Serves 6

1 quantity Sweet Pastry (see page 188)
2 lb (900 g) firm apples, such as Fuji, golden
    delicious, or Granny Smith
⅓ cup soft light brown sugar
1 teaspoon ground cinnamon
¼ teaspoon each freshly grated nutmeg and
    ground cloves
1 medium farm-fresh egg white
2 tablespoons semolina
2 tablespoons superfine sugar

For the mincemeat ice cream:

1 cup mixed dried fruits, such as golden
    raisins, currants, raisins, and chopped
    candied peel
5 tablespoons dark rum
2½ cups milk
6 medium farm-fresh egg yolks
¼ cup superfine sugar
1 cup heavy cream
⅓ cup toasted chopped almonds

For the ice cream, put the mixed dried fruits and rum together into a bowl. Cover and set to one side for a few hours to let the fruits soak up all the rum. Bring the milk to a boil in a pan. Whisk the egg yolks and sugar together in a bowl until pale and creamy. Pour on the hot milk, whisk together well, and return the mixture to the pan. Cook over a gentle heat, stirring, until it lightly coats the back of a wooden spoon. Stir in the cream and leave to cool; then chill in the refrigerator for about 1 hour until really cold. Now you can either churn the mixture in an ice cream machine, adding the rum-soaked fruits and toasted, chopped almonds a few minutes before the end, or pour it into a shallow plastic box and leave in the freezer until almost firm. If doing the latter, scrape the mixture into a food processor and whizz it until smooth – this will break down all the ice crystals in the mixture. Scrape the mixture back into the box, return it to the freezer, and leave until almost firm. Repeat the whizzing process once more; then stir in the rum-soaked fruits and toasted, chopped almonds and leave in the freezer until really firm or until required.

For the apple tarts, preheat the oven to 400°F (200°C). Quarter the apples, core and then peel them. Slice thickly into a bowl and stir in the sugar and the spices. Divide the pastry into 6 equal pieces and, on a lightly floured board, roll each one out into a 7 inch (18 cm) round. Brush each round with a little of the unbeaten egg white and then sprinkle 1 teaspoon of the semolina into the center of each one, leaving a 2 inch (5 cm) border around the edge free. Pile the apple mixture into the center and then fold the edges of the pastry over the fruit, leaving some of the fruit showing in the middle and pleating the pastry as you go to keep it in place.

Carefully lift the tarts onto a lightly buttered baking sheet and chill for 30 minutes. Brush the edges of the tarts with more of the unbeaten egg white and then sprinkle with the superfine sugar. Bake the tarts for 25–30 minutes until the pastry is golden and the apples are cooked. Slide onto dessert plates and serve with scoops of the mincemeat ice cream.

MACERATED STRAWBERRIES
with basil and white pepper ice cream

An intriguing combination this, but strawberries, basil, and pepper really do work together. Talking about pepper, why is it so difficult to buy white peppercorns? The only place that I ever seem to have success is the local Indian grocer's shop. Supermarkets everywhere, please take heed and stock them now!

Serves 6-8

1½–2 lb (675–900 g) strawberries

2 tablespoons superfine sugar

1 tablespoon eau de fraise, eau de vie,
    or Kirsch

12 fresh basil leaves, very finely shredded

For the white pepper ice cream:

1 teaspoon white peppercorns

2½ cups milk

6 medium farm-fresh egg yolks

5 tablespoons superfine sugar

1 cup heavy cream

For the ice cream, crush the peppercorns in a mortar and pestle or in a mug using the end of a rolling pin. Tip them into a tea strainer or small fine sieve and sift away all the fine powder so that you are left with just very small crumbs of pepper. Bring the milk to a boil in a pan. Whisk the egg yolks and sugar together in a bowl until pale and creamy. Pour on the hot milk, whisk together well, and return the mixture to the pan. Cook over a gentle heat, stirring, until it lightly coats the back of a wooden spoon. Pour into a bowl and leave to cool. Then stir in the cream and pepper and chill in the refrigerator for about 1 hour until the mixture is really cold. Now you can either churn the mixture in an ice cream machine or pour it into a shallow plastic box and leave it in the freezer until almost firm. If doing the latter, scrape the mixture into a food processor and whizz it until smooth – this will break down all the ice crystals in the mixture. Scrape the mixture back into the box, return to the freezer, and leave until almost firm. Repeat the whizzing process once more and then leave in the freezer until really firm or until required.

Hull the strawberries and slice them in half into a bowl. Stir in the sugar, eau de fraise, eau de vie, or Kirsch, and basil. Cover and chill in the refrigerator for 15–30 minutes. Serve the strawberries in dessert bowls with scoops of the white pepper ice cream.

MY MUM'S PANCAKES

with a choice of preserves

A lovely dessert or perfect for afternoon tea. A little clotted cream wouldn't go amiss either. The preserves make far more than you need for one sitting but also taste great on toast or ordinary warm scones.

Serves 4

For the pancakes:

⅔ cup self-rising flour

1 teaspoon baking powder

¼ cup granulated sugar

1 farm-fresh egg

⅔ cup milk

a little butter, to serve

For the whisky and rhubarb preserve:

3 lb (1.5 kg) wild or cultivated rhubarb

4 cups sugar

finely grated zest of 1 lemon

¾ cup best Islay whisky

For Aunty Ulla's no-cook marmalade:

8 oz (225 g) dried apricots, washed

1 lemon

2 oranges

2 cups superfine sugar

First make the preserves. For the whisky and rhubarb preserve, cut off either end of each piece of rhubarb and wipe the stalks clean with a cloth – there's no need to peel them. Cut them into 1 inch (2.5 cm) long chunks. Layer the rhubarb and sugar in a large, deep bowl or dish and leave to stand for 24 hours, by which time the sugar should have changed into a liquid state. Pour the sugary liquid into a preserving pan and add the grated lemon zest. Bring to a boil and boil briskly for 30 minutes. Now add the rhubarb and boil for another 30 minutes. Take the pan off the heat and stir in the whisky. Place the pan near a hot oven or an open fire and leave it to stand for another 30 minutes. Then spoon the preserve into sterilized jars, cover with wax discs and seal.

For Aunty Ulla's no-cook marmalade, you will need to soak the dried apricots overnight. The next day, drain them and grind them in a meat grinder or give them a whizz in a food processor. Scrub the lemon and the oranges; then drop them into a pan of boiling water and scald for 1 minute. Remove and, when cooled slightly, cut them in half and squeeze out the juice. Grind or whizz the flesh and mix this with the juice, the sugar, and the ground apricots. Pack the mixture in a large sterilized jar. You can use it straightaway but it's best kept for 2–3 days to let the flavor mature.

For the pancakes, sift the flour and baking powder into a bowl and stir in the granulated sugar. Whisk the egg and then stir it into the dry ingredients – it is very important that you don't beat it in. Then whisk in enough milk to make a batter which has the consistency of heavy cream.

Heat a smooth, cast-iron griddle over a medium–high heat. Test the heat by sprinkling the griddle with a little flour. If it browns straightaway, it is too hot. If it takes a few seconds before it browns, then it's perfect.

Drop 3 tablespoonfuls of the batter, spaced a little apart, onto the griddle. When bubbles appear on the tops of the pancakes and they are golden brown underneath – about 2–3 minutes – turn them over using a spatula, and cook for another 2 minutes until golden brown on the other side. Lift them off onto a plate and cover with a cloth. Keep warm while you cook the rest. You should make about 12 pancakes. Then simply serve them spread with a little butter and some preserve.

FRUIT SCONE AND BUTTER PUDDINGS

The idea for this came from my noticing that an average scone fits perfectly inside a 3 inch (7.5 cm) ramekin. Don't ask how that particular thought occurred to me – many and mysterious are the ways of a chef's brain! However, scones do make excellent individual puddings which can be made up in advance and reheated if you wish. The rest of the scones are fantastic split and served with strawberry jam and clotted cream, or just butter.

Serves 6

⅓ cup golden raisins

⅓ cup dried apricots, chopped into
   small pieces

¼ cup good whisky

1 vanilla bean

1¼ cups milk

1¼ cups heavy cream

5 medium farm-fresh egg yolks

¼ cup superfine sugar

5 tablespoons butter for spreading

4 tablespoons warm sieved apricot jam

For the fruit scones:

2 cups self-rising flour

½ teaspoon salt

1 teaspoon baking powder

3 tablespoons unsalted butter

⅓ cup raisins, or currants, golden raisins,
   chopped dates, etc.

3 tablespoons superfine sugar

⅔ cup milk

beaten egg or milk, to glaze

Place the golden raisins, apricots and whisky in a small bowl, cover and leave to soak, overnight if possible or for a minimum of 2 hours.

The next day, make the scones. Slide a baking sheet into the oven and preheat it to 450°F (230°C). Sift the flour, salt, and baking powder into a bowl and then rub in the butter until the mixture looks like fine breadcrumbs. Stir in the dried fruits and the sugar. Make a well in the center and stir in enough milk to give a soft dough – make sure the mixture is not too dry or the scones will end up like little rocks! Turn the mixture out onto a lightly floured surface and knead briefly to remove any cracks from the mixture. Then gently roll it out (or pat it out with your hands if you prefer) until the dough is about ¾ inch (2 cm) thick. Cut out 10–12 rounds using a 5 cm (2 inch) cutter dipped in flour. Brush with egg or milk and place on the hot baking sheet. Bake toward the top of the oven for 8–10 minutes until the scones are well risen and brown. Transfer to a wire rack and leave to cool. Reduce the oven temperature to 350°F (180°C).

Cut the vanilla bean in half and scrape out the seeds into a pan. Add the milk and the cream and bring to a boil very slowly. Remove the vanilla bean.

Cream the egg yolks and sugar together in a bowl and then whisk in two-thirds of the hot milk and cream. Mix together well, then return to the pan containing the remaining milk and cream mix. Cook over a gentle heat, stirring all the time, until the mixture lightly coats the back of a wooden spoon. Pour into a pitcher and set aside.

Very thinly slice the baked top and bottom off 6 of the scones and discard. These are the scones you will be using for the puddings. (Store the remaining scones in an airtight container; they will keep for 3 days.) Cut each of the 6 scones into 3 slices and spread each slice quite heavily with butter.

Place one scone slice in the bottom of a greased 3 inch (7.5 cm) ramekin and sprinkle over a few of the soaked golden raisins and apricots. Pour over a little of the custard mix to cover. Repeat twice more so that the ramekin is filled to the top. Repeat the process with 5 more ramekins. Set aside for ¾–1 hour.

Sit the ramekins in a roasting pan and pour in hot water until it comes halfway up the sides of the dishes. Bake for 40 minutes until set and lightly golden. Remove the ramekins from the roasting pan. Brush the puddings with a little of the warmed apricot jam and serve straightaway.

HOT TODDIE SOUFFLÉS

While mucking about with the idea of using hot toddie flavorings in various desserts, I struck on the idea of the hot toddie soufflé. Out of the range of ideas I tried – mousse, tart, ice cream, etc. – this was by far the best. So here's the recipe for your delectation. As with all soufflés, butter the mold well and don't overwhisk the egg whites.

Serves 6

a little butter for greasing

3 tablespoons superfine sugar, plus extra for dusting

¼ cup whisky

1 teaspoon finely grated lemon zest

1 tablespoon lemon juice

3 whole cloves

1¼ cups milk

3 medium farm-fresh egg yolks

1½ tablespoons all-purpose flour

1½ tablespoons cornstarch

4 tablespoons clear honey

6 medium farm-fresh egg whites

confectioners' sugar, to decorate

Slide a baking sheet onto the middle shelf of the oven and preheat it to 425°F (220°C). Grease six 3 inch (7.5 cm) ramekins with butter, making sure that you take it right up to the top of the rim, and dust them out with some of the superfine sugar.

Put the whisky, lemon zest, lemon juice, and cloves into a small pan and leave over a low heat. Pour the milk into another pan and bring it up to a boil. Mix the egg yolks, the 3 tablespoons superfine sugar, flour, and cornstarch together in a bowl until smooth. Whisk in the boiling milk, return the mixture to the pan and cook over a gentle heat, stirring every now and then, for 10 minutes so that you cook out the taste of the flour. Strain the whisky mixture into the custard. Add 1 tablespoon of the honey and whisk together well.

Whisk the egg whites in a large clean bowl into soft peaks. Gradually whisk in the rest of the honey to make a soft meringue. Lightly whisk one-quarter of the honey meringue into the custard to loosen it slightly, then carefully fold in the remainder. Spoon the mixture into the prepared ramekins and level the tops; then run the tip of a knife around the inside edge of each dish to release the mixture. Slide the ramekins onto the baking sheet and bake for 10–12 minutes until the soufflés are well risen, browned, and doubled in height but still slightly wobbly. Quickly lift them onto small dessert plates, dust with confectioners' sugar and serve straightaway.

BASICS

MARINATED VEGETABLE STOCK

This stock freezes well and the ingredients are always reasonably easy to get. Freeze it in small tubs so that you can defrost the required quantity as and when you need it.

**Makes about
5 cups**

1 large onion
1 leek, cleaned
2 stalks celery
1 fennel bulb (optional)
4 large carrots

1 head garlic, cut across its equator
8 white peppercorns
1 teaspoon pink peppercorns (optional)
1 teaspoon coriander seeds
1 piece star anise
1 fresh bay leaf
¾ cup mixed fresh herbs
1¼ cups dry white wine

Chop all the vegetables into ½ inch (1 cm) dice. Place in a large pan and cover with water. Add the garlic, peppercorns, coriander seeds, star anise, and bay leaf. Bring to the boil and simmer for 8 minutes. Add the fresh herbs and simmer for 3 minutes more. Now add the white wine and remove from the heat. Cover and leave to marinate somewhere cool for 48 hours. Then strain through a fine sieve and use immediately, or freeze and use within 6 weeks.

FISH STOCK

Good fish stock should form a slight jelly consistency. In the summer, it's best to freeze stock immediately but in the winter it will keep for 48 hours in the refrigerator.

Makes about 1 ¼ cups

1 ½ lb (675 g) fish bones, preferably sole, turbot, or brill

5 cups cold water

½ medium-size onion, finely diced

1 white of leek, finely diced

1 celery stalk, finely diced

6 white peppercorns

½ fresh bay leaf

¼ cup fresh herbs, such as chervil, parsley, tarragon, and cilantro

1 tablespoon olive oil

1 ¼ cups dry white wine

Soak the fish bones in cold water for half an hour. Drain, wash and roughly chop.

In a medium-size saucepan, gently sweat all of the finely diced vegetables, peppercorns, bay leaf, and herbs in the olive oil until soft, but without coloring them. Add the white wine and boil until nearly dry. Now add the fish bones and stir to coat. Pour over enough cold water just to cover the mixture (about 5 cups). Bring it to a boil, skim and then simmer for about 18 minutes (do not let it boil). Remove it from the heat and leave to stand until cool (this takes about 3-4 hours).

Once cooled, pour the stock through a sieve or colander, then pass it through a fine sieve into a tall container. Place in the refrigerator and leave it overnight to let it settle.

The next day, skim off any scum that has settled on the top, then spoon off all the clear jellied stock, which should then be frozen until needed.

You may notice some white gunge at the bottom of the container. This should not be considered edible and should be discarded.

CHICKEN STOCK

There is nothing to compare with a good homemade chicken stock and it is invaluable in the kitchen. Use uncooked chicken carcasses, not ones left over from the Sunday roast, to ensure you get that lovely fresh flavor.

Makes about 5 ¼ cups

3 chicken carcasses, skin and fat removed

1 large carrot, quartered

2 medium leeks, cleaned

2 stalks celery, halved lengthwise

1 unpeeled onion, quartered

1 small head garlic, cut across its equator

6 white peppercorns

1 fresh bay leaf

1 sprig of fresh thyme

¼ cup fresh parsley or tarragon stalks

Place the carcasses in a large pan that they only half fill. Just cover with about 9½ cups of cold water and bring to a boil, skimming off any scum as it rises to the surface. Skim off any fat, then place the rest of the ingredients in a thick layer over the top of the carcasses. Adjust the heat to a simmer and leave to cook for 3–4 hours, during which time the vegetables will act like a filter, absorbing all the gunk and leaving you with a crystal clear stock. Taste the stock every now and then while it's cooking. When you notice that the flavor stops improving, your stock is ready.

Strain the stock into another pan through a colander, and then once more through a chinois or fine sieve into a tall container or large pitcher. Cover and leave to cool, then chill in the refrigerator overnight. The next day, skim any fat off the surface and use as required, or freeze to use later.

BEEF STOCK

Making a good beef stock is a time-consuming business as it has to be simmered for 8 hours, but it's a must for jus sauces – namely those made only of well-reduced stocks. It gives them plenty of body and prevents them from being too watery.

Makes 5 cups

10 lb (4.5 kg) beef knuckle bones
2 large carrots, cut into 1 inch (2.5 cm) pieces
2 large unpeeled onions, cut into 8 wedges
2 large leeks, cleaned and cut into 1 inch (2.5 cm) pieces
2 stalks celery, cut into 1 inch (2.5 cm) pieces
1 head garlic, cut across its equator

¼ cup fresh parsley or tarragon stalks
1 fresh bay leaf
1 large sprig of fresh thyme
12 black peppercorns
3 plum tomatoes, quartered
2 tablespoons tomato paste
1¼ cups red wine
1 pig's trotter
1 lb (450 g) shin of beef

Preheat the oven to 400°F (200°C). Place the beef bones in a large roasting pan, slide them into the hot oven, and roast for about 1 hour until well browned. Tip off the marrow fat and reserve.

Heat a large stock pot until very hot and add 3 tablespoons of the marrow fat (which should smoke as soon as it hits the hot pan). Add all the vegetables (except the tomatoes), the garlic, herbs, and peppercorns, and stir over a high heat until well browned – it is important to achieve a good, dark color, but without burning.

Add the tomatoes and the tomato paste and cook until the tomatoes have reduced to a thick pulp. Add the wine and boil until it has almost all disappeared. Now add the roasted beef bones, the pig's trotter, and the shin of beef, and cover with cold water. Bring to a boil, skimming the scum off the surface as it appears, then reduce the heat so that the liquid barely trembles and leave to simmer for 8 hours, or preferably overnight.

Strain the stock into another pan and leave to cool. Once cold, skim off any fat, strain once more through a chinois or fine sieve into another pan, and bring back to a boil. Continue to boil until reduced by half and then leave to cool. Use or freeze as required.

BALSAMIC VINEGAR SYRUP

This process intensifies the flavor of the vinegar and also makes it thick and syrupy so that it looks great when drizzled over a plate, especially with a little oil. It is excellent drizzled over roasted vegetables, a Parma ham salad, arugula leaves, or anything vaguely Italian. When you're making it, ensure the kitchen is well ventilated as the vinegary fumes can make your eyes water. And use middle-of-the-road vinegar for this recipe, not your best 10-year-old vinegar.

1 bottle balsamic vinegar

Bring the vinegar to a boil in a pan and leave it to simmer quite vigorously until it has reduced by about half and become thick and syrupy. Watch it toward the end as you don't want it to go too far and burn. Leave to cool, then store in an airtight bottle. It will keep indefinitely.

CLARIFIED BUTTER

Clarified butter is the oily part of the butter, that is, without the buttermilk and is excellent for frying potatoes to give them a rich buttery color. You can buy it ready prepared in Indian delicatessens (as *ghee*).

Makes about scant 1 cup   *generous 1 cup butter*

In a small pan, melt the butter on a low heat. Let it stand for a few minutes until all the oil rises to the top, then skim off the scum that has risen to the surface. Pour off the clear oil into a small bowl, leaving behind the milky-white solids which will have collected at the bottom. Discard the milky-white solids. The oil will keep in the refrigerator for 2–3 days.

TOMATOES CONCASSÉES

Peeled, seeded, and neatly diced tomatoes that have had all their acidic juices removed can be used for all sorts of salads and sauces. Their success will depend on the quality of the plum tomatoes you use.

firm, ripe, plum tomatoes

Remove the skins of the tomatoes. You can do this in one of two ways:

Hot water: Cut a little, shallow cross in the top of each tomato. Place them in a bowl and cover with boiling water. Leave for about 30 seconds, drain and cover with cold water. The skins should come off quite easily.

Naked flame: Spear the tomatoes onto a fork or skewer. Place them near a naked flame – the gas burner of your stove or a blowtorch – and turn them until the skins start to blacken and blister. Then peel.

Cut the peeled tomatoes into quarters. Scoop out the seeds and cut the flesh into very neat ¼ inch (5 mm) dice. They are best used immediately but will keep refrigerated for up to 24 hours.

HOME-DRIED TOMATOES

Makes 24 pieces

12 large, ripe plum tomatoes
Maldon or sea salt and freshly ground
* white pepper*

¼ cup olive oil, plus extra for preserving
1 sprig of fresh basil or thyme
1 clove garlic, crushed

Preheat the oven to 225°F (110°C). Slice the tomatoes in half lengthwise and remove the little green "eyes" from the stalk ends. Place the tomatoes cut-side up on a baking sheet and sprinkle with crushed salt and 12 turns of the pepper mill. Drizzle over the ¼ cup olive oil.

Place the tomatoes in the oven and leave for 8 hours, by which time they should have shrunk to half their original size but not browned. Turn them over and leave for another 4 hours or until they are nice and firm.

Remove them from the oven and leave to go cold. Then pack them with the basil or thyme and garlic into a sterilized jar that holds about 2½ cups and cover in olive oil. Seal and store in the refrigerator for up to 3 weeks.

ROASTED RED BELL PEPPERS

Use large, ripe, red bell peppers here. The secret of success is to get the skin of the pepper really blackened without burning the flesh underneath.

6 large red bell peppers
olive oil
1 clove garlic

1 sprig of fresh thyme
1 fresh bay leaf

There are three ways of skinning peppers:

Oven roasting: Preheat the oven to 475°F (240°C). Place the peppers directly on the oven rack and put a baking sheet on the rack underneath to collect any dripping juices. Roast the bell peppers, turning them once or twice, for 10–15 minutes, or until their skins are blistered and blackened.

Broiling: Preheat your broiler to its highest setting. Rub a little olive oil over the outside of the peppers, place them on the rack of the broiler pan and broil them, turning them as they color, until they are blackened all over.

Naked flame: Spear the peppers onto a fork or skewer. Place them near a naked flame – the gas burner of your stove or a blowtorch – and turn them until they are blackened all over.

Drop the peppers into a plastic bag and seal, or wrap tightly in plastic wrap, and leave to cool. Unwrap the peppers, cut them open, and scoop out the seeds. Then carefully peel off the skins, which will come away quite easily, and use the flesh as required.

If you don't want to use the peppers straightaway, pack them into a sterilized jar with the garlic, thyme, and bay leaf. Cover with olive oil, seal and store them in the refrigerator for up to 2 weeks.

HERB OIL

If you prize color and fragrance in your meals, this is for you. You could also make it with individual herbs instead of a mixture. Chive oil retains its grassy color better than any other, while the aroma of basil oil is unmistakable and guaranteed to lift your mood. Herb oil has a fabulous color and makes a great garnish to many dishes.

Makes about 1 ¼ cups

¾ cup mixed fresh herbs, such as chives, parsley, chervil, tarragon, and dill
1 ¼ cups olive oil

Drop the herbs into a pan of heavily salted boiling water and leave for just 10 seconds to set the color. Drain and refresh under cold water to stop the cooking process, then drain and wring out well in a clean dish towel. Chop up roughly and place in a blender with the oil. Blitz for 2–3 minutes. Pour into a sterilized bottle, seal and refrigerate. Shake before using and keep for up to 1 week.

CHILI OIL

This stuff is mega spicy but, used sparingly, it imparts a wonderful glow to many dishes and looks stunning drizzled around the edge of a plate as garnish.

Makes about 1 ¼ cups

2 oz (50 g) ripe, red chili peppers, preferably Scotch bonnets
1 large red bell pepper, seeded
1 ¼ cups sunflower oil

Slice the chilies in half lengthwise and roughly chop the red bell pepper. Place in a pan with the oil, carefully bring to a boil, and leave to simmer gently for 10 minutes. Remove from the heat and leave to cool.

Once cold, transfer to a sealable plastic or glass container and leave in a cool place for 2–3 weeks. Then pour the oil through a fine sieve into a bottle and use as required.

CURRY OIL

This oil has a wonderful amber color and aromatic taste which can be used for cooking dishes of a similar nature, as well as for garnishing numerous spicy dishes.

Makes about 1 ¼ cups

1 ¼ cups olive oil
1 teaspoon coriander seeds
1 teaspoon cumin seeds

½ inch (1 cm) piece fresh ginger root, bruised and then very finely chopped
1 clove garlic
1 tablespoon good-quality curry paste

Heat 2 tablespoons of the oil in a pan. Add the spices, ginger, and garlic and cook over a medium heat for about 1 minute. Add the curry paste and cook for another 30 seconds. Add the rest of the oil and simmer for 5 minutes. Leave to cool and then transfer to a bottle, seal and store in a cool, dark place until needed. Shake before using.

LOBSTER OR SHELLFISH OIL

This is quite extravagant but does add a wonderful flavor to many fish and seafood dishes. It's also a great way of making use of all those shells that are usually just discarded.

Makes about 1 ¼ cups

6 oz (175 g) lobster or langoustine shells
1 ½ cups sunflower oil
1 tiny piece broken star anise
3 white peppercorns
2 inch (5 cm) piece carrot, peeled and diced

2 shallots, diced
2 inch (5 cm) piece celery, diced
2 cloves garlic
¼ cup mixed fresh herbs such as, parsley, thyme and tarragon
½ teaspoon tomato paste
¼ cup dry white wine

Crush the shells and drain away any liquid. Heat 4 tablespoons of the oil in a pan. Add the shells, star anise, and white peppercorns, and fry over a medium heat for about 15 minutes, stirring every now and then. Add all the remaining ingredients, except the oil, and cook until the wine has evaporated. Add the rest of the oil and leave to simmer for 45 minutes. Remove from the heat and leave to stand for 24 hours. Strain through a muslin-lined sieve, transfer to a bottle and seal. This will keep in the refrigerator for about 1 month.

SWEET PASTRY

Makes about 1 lb (450 g),
enough to line one 10 inch (25 cm) pie
pans or 6 (4 inch) (10 cm) tartlet pans

¾ cup unsalted butter, at room temperature
¼ cup superfine sugar

a pinch of Maldon or sea salt
generous 2 cups all-purpose flour
1 medium farm-fresh egg yolk
1 tablespoon cold water

Cream the butter, sugar, and salt together in a bowl until light and fluffy (you can do this with an electric mixer or in a food processor). Add 6 tablespoons of the flour and mix in. Now add the egg yolk and slowly mix in the rest of the flour a spoonful at a time until it is all incorporated. Add the water and mix for another 15 seconds.

Turn the dough onto a lightly floured surface and knead briefly (3 or 4 times) until smooth. Cover in plastic wrap and chill in the refrigerator for at least 3 hours before using.

Slide a baking sheet into the oven and preheat it to 400°F (200°C). Remove the pastry from the refrigerator and knead briefly once more until smooth.

For one 10 inch (25 cm) pastry shell: Roll out the pastry to a thickness of about ⅛ inch (3 mm) on a floured surface and use to line a lightly greased pie pan. Leave the excess pastry overhanging and line with wax paper and baking beans. Chill in the refrigerator for 15 minutes. Now slide the shell onto the baking sheet and bake for 11 minutes. Remove the paper and beans and bake the shell for another 9 minutes more or until the pastry is lightly browned. Neatly slice away the overhanging pastry and leave the shell to cool and then use when required.

For six tartlet cases: Cut the pastry into 6 even pieces. Roll out and use to line 6 lightly greased 4 inch (10 cm) tartlet pans. Line with wax paper and beans, chill for 15 minutes, and then bake as before.

STOCK SYRUP

Makes about 5¼ cups

4½ cups granulated sugar
4¼ cups water

Put the sugar and water into a medium-size pan and place over a high heat. Bring to a boil, stirring from time to time. Leave the syrup to simmer for 5 minutes before skimming off any impurities that may have risen to the surface. Leave to cool and use as required.

INDEX

Page references to illustrations are in *italic*